FACING
THE
WORLD
WITH
SOUL

STUDIES
IN IMAGINATION

A series edited in collaboration with
The Institute for the Study of Imagination

•

The Planets Within, Thomas Moore
Facing the World with Soul, Robert Sardello
Archetypal Imagination, Noel Cobb
Book of the Heart, Andrés Rodríguez

FACING
THE
WORLD
WITH
SOUL

BY

ROBERT SARDELLO

LINDISFARNE PRESS

Published by
Lindisfarne Press
RR 4, Box 94 A-1,
Hudson, New York 12534

ISBN: 0-940262-46-0

Library of Congress Cataloging-in-Publication Data
Sardello, Robert J. 1942-
    Facing the world with soul: the reimagination of modern life
Robert Sardello.
        p. cm.
    Includes bibliographical references.
    ISBN 0-940262-46-0 (pbk.)
    1. Conduct of life.   2. Soul.   I. Title.
BF637.C5S27   1991
158'.1—dc20   91-31727
                                                                                        CIP

10 9 8 7 6 5 4 3

Book design and typography by Studio 31

Manufactured in the United States of America

CONTENTS

For
KAREN, MARC and LUKE

Foreword

On this morning of the beginning of my forty-eighth year I begin a series of letters to you, meditations that could be called "Facing the World With Soul." These letters issue from a soul in pain in intimacy with the world in which we live and are addressed to you, dear reader, whose soul may be undergoing similar experiences. Thinking that the suffering I have felt for as long as I can remember arose from some unknown cause sent me in search of healing, beginning with training as a psychologist. Besides having undergone no less than five different kinds of psychotherapy, I have attempted a myriad of other healing techniques from acupuncture to crystal healing to radionics to past life regression to astrological counseling; no need to name the rest. How long it has taken to realize that there is another side to suffering than that felt so personally! How long it has taken to come to the point of seeing that the question of soul pain *is not what to do about it but what to do with it*. Pain, imperceptible psychic and emotional pain, is the invaluable medium through which the world can be regenerated. What a wondrous mystery we encounter here if this proposition holds even *a semblance* of truth. I am suggesting that political, social, economic, ecological, and technological programs (and all other imaginable kinds of programs) will not alter the condition of the world one wit; they only rearrange what is already given into new patterns into which we are inserted as onlookers, strangers.

If the mentality of programs that attempt to alter the world is impotent because it seeks to do something about rather than with pain, even more impotent are the so-called helping professions that try to do something about inner,

9

individual pain. I can now imagine nothing more detrimental to the world than the illusory success of removing pain of a psychic nature, for to do so obliterates completely the presence of soul that might be available as the most vitalizing regenerative resource for the outer world. At this point, dear friend, you might think my initial wanderings crazed beyond belief. Please bear with me a short time longer and you shall see for yourself that I am trying to open a door, not to shut them all.

Consider an instance of emotional pain — anger. Quite ordinarily we take anger to be attached to someone; someone or something has wounded us and we feel anger toward the person or the thing. But what is anger? As long as anger is felt as attached to someone, then we are automatically in an attitude that something must be done about it. This attitude of doing something about it — venting it, raging, discussing it, finding out who "really" is the source — bypasses the anger as a quality of soul. We might call that quality pure force. Mythically, we might imagine anger as Mars. Mars is not angry at anybody; that is just who he is. And when we feel anger, another person or thing is not the cause of the anger but its occasion. The work, then, is to detach the anger from supposed connections, which always make us live in the past, and to experience that quality of soul called pure force. Assuredly, this takes practice and discipline. The result of such discipline, however, does not take the form of what to do about the anger, but rather of letting what to do with the anger appear in the imagination. I do not mean go out and chop wood, but rather let that pure force of the soul become a mode of perception of the outer world. I am also not saying be angry at the world, but see the world through, by way of, the quality of pure force. Then, gradually, it becomes apparent that anger, pure force, is pure vitality. Because this soul quality has been given attention, that very same quality begins to show itself in the world. This is not projection in the now common sense of the term, but it is projection in the alchemical sense, a utilization of image in order to evoke a similar image from the world itself, the projection of apprehension through similars. Most importantly, the soul quality of pure force that now begins to show itself in the world is really there. It was there before the act of projection, though in a confused way, what the alchemists called the "massa confusa." Through the ongoing exercise of this conscious, imaginal seeing through the things of the world, the world soul regenerates.

In the following letters I want to engage in this practice of seeing the world through soul in order to come to the soul of the world. Sometimes I will suggest particular exercises that may be of help if you find yourself interested in this way of living but also find yourself baffled concerning how to proceed. In ancient times exercises were a central part of the mystery schools necessary to bring about new forms of perception. Today the mystery school is the world as it is given and available to everyone, and initiation into soul a daily task. Further, there are no set exercises; we must all come to our own. Consequently, the following letters often do not indicate any particular exercise at all; I simply present images of the world, images that come from this form of discipline of working with soul as the medium of enlivening the soul of the world, and I leave to your own imagination the task of finding practices suitable for you.

The subject matter of these letters varies, but the focus is always on the world in which we presently live, things that we are all concerned about, particularly those aspects of the outer world that trouble us in these times — money, health, education, environment, nutrition, spirit, the city, addictions, technology. Thus, when speaking of world I do not mean nature, but rather the artifactual world that appears soulless. This world is so prevalent that as soon as I mention the focus of these letters you may not wish to continue, for we already feel inundated with popular talk about such matters. If anything you may want relief by escaping into the exotic. I accept the challenge by suggesting that our ordinary pain-filled world holds mysteries if we can but learn to perceive soul through the medium of soul.

My aim is to encourage a kind of conscious image state that curbs the problem-attacking mode of facing the world. Instead, I encourage you to face the world through whatever pathologies you are gifted with and to work to be acutely aware of these same pathologies also in every aspect of the world itself, as if something is trying to come to birth, a new imaginative consciousness that is fully awake and fully alive.

With all things that one finds oneself drawn to so strongly that years of life are given and everything sacrificed in their pursuit, there can be found an underlying myth, a story larger than oneself that reveals the essence of the work in which one has been engaged. These letters and their concerns seem to be connected with the Grail legend, most completely told in Wolfram von Eschenbach's *Parzival.*

I take the Grail to be the soul of the world. Parzival, early in life and filled with innocence, goes in quest of the Grail. His adventures help him acquire experience, gradually. Early on he encounters the Grail but does not ask the crucial question he is destined to ask — "Brother, what ails thee?" Only after going through many painful experiences does he again come to the Grail. But that is not the end nor the point of his travails. He is led into a fight with his brother, whom he does not know to be his brother. At the moment when death is imminent, the two recognize each other, and Parzival leads his brother to the Grail. If forty-eight years of the experience of searching for the soul of the world, of struggling to gain awareness of the inner qualities of the outer world, is of any significance at all, it is to engage known and unknown friends to come and look for themselves.

I have had the extreme fortune of being surrounded for years by people who place value in soul and whose lives are a practice of living in soul. All that I have learned comes from them. In truth, without the circumstances that led to these lifelong connections, I would be a crazy academic psychologist still doing meaningless experiments. The depth of gratitude I feel toward Dr. Gail Thomas can only be known in the intimacy of my own soul, and this acknowledgment does no justice to the significance of her unending encouragement and support as well as thoughtfulness and care. We have worked together for twenty years, and this book contains as many of her insights as my own. Dr. James Hillman has had, among other qualities, the exceptional ability to really hear where this work was tending, even before I myself had any real idea of what I was doing. For many years he has encouraged and even pushed me to continue the work when no one else would give it a second glance. Dr. Louise Cowan is chiefly responsible for the awakening and shaping of my imagination. An astounding literary critic and teacher, Dr. Cowan made me see that imagination is a mode of knowledge. For years we had remarkable conversations in which she worked the magic of transforming a narrow, opinionated soul into one with some flexibility; no easy task. Dr. Donald Cowan is a visionary and a prophet, an extremely rare individual who has the capacity for grasping the whole, for astute analysis that never loses the quality of the whole, and for imagination as a creative force. It was through him — a physicist who speaks as a poet — that I came to realize the importance of the world, of culture, that I came to realize the true nature of the crises we now face and the directions we need to take through our time into the coming age. These people are truly the co-authors of this work.

Then, there are invaluable friends who have continually encouraged my efforts over the years. These friends include Robert Romanyshyn, Joanne Stroud, Joe Guy, and especially Cheryl Beckworth. Without their presence I would have stopped thinking and writing years ago. Randolph Severson, an editorial genius, went through the manuscript and made most helpful revisions. Robert Palmer thoroughly edited the first version of this work, a true act of love.

I wish to express my indebtedness to The Dallas Institute of Humanities and Culture, my home for the past ten years. Through the most able leadership of Gail Thomas this enterprise has flourished in the heart of a city that at first did not know what to make of a group of people who wished to bring the life of thought, imagination, and inspiration out of the narrow academic world and into the city. The benefits to the city have proved salutary. I thank all of those who support the efforts of the Institute, and in particular I wish to thank the wonderful students from whom I never cease learning.

Special thanks is due Christopher Bamford for taking on the task of seeing this work through publication.

*
**

LETTER I

The Soul of the World

DEAR FRIEND,

This first letter intends to lay a groundwork for the letters that follow. The purpose of these letters is to serve as an antidote to the subjectivizing tendencies of a psychological culture. The more psychologically aware we become, it seems, the further away from the world we find ourselves. It may well be that psychology and psychotherapy are oriented toward the conquest of soul rather than toward and entry into soul wisdom. By soul wisdom I mean the development of a capacity for self-knowledge in conjunction with an objective sense of the inner qualities of the outer world. The capacity for this conjunction leads to a new image consciousness that "sees through" events, both inner and outer, finding a circulation going on between them in which a constant recreation of both the human being and the world takes place. This circulating force or power I shall call soul, and to make clear that what I am calling soul has little to do with individual life alone, by soul I shall always imply *the soul of the world* as a way of referring to the inseparable conjunction of individual and world; and further, this is always a conjunction in depth.

The impulse leading to the desire to bring about a correction of a one-sidedness of the work of psychology issues from the observation that the place where therapy needs to be practiced has shifted from the isolated chamber of the psychotherapist's office to the world. Medicine, education, money, food, energy, media, technology, religion, buildings, economics — all of those organizing forms

15

that together ought to make culture no longer do so but instead are making a pathological civilization. The new symptoms are fragmentation, specialization, expertise, depression, inflation, cruelty, hardness, violence, and absence of beauty. Our buildings are anorectic, our business paranoid, detached, and abstract, our technology manic. These symptoms indicate the loss of the containment characteristic of the vessel of soul. The work of psychology, it seems to me, consists of a re-evaluation of the domains of the modern world in terms of metaphor, image, story, and dream. The things of the world have stories to tell when the fragmentations of culture are looked upon as analogous to dream fragments through which the depth of the world seeks to be remembered.

The background for approaching the world in this manner is from archetypal psychology as practiced by James Hillman. Archetypally, this approach derives from Sophia, who stands as the world soul, she through whom everything in the outer world has qualities of interiority. Who is Sophia? This question shall be the main focus of this letter, and what follows is an attempt to trace her activities in the shaping of the present world. We shall find the most ancient interwoven with the new. We shall avoid on the one hand all regression to the past and on the other hand all judgment and criticism and all prescriptions for improving the present state of world activities that do not imply a radical alteration of consciousness.

There are many myths and stories of Sophia, all of which point to her as creator of the world. Pistis Sophia she is called, meaning ever faithful. Faithfulness describes her constant presence within the things of the world where she silently waits with the gift that no one wants or recognizes: renewal and regeneration of the material world. In the gnostic myth Sophia is situated at the thirteenth Aeon, the archetypal world nearest to the fullness, the pleroma. She looks above and sees a radiant light and falls in love with the light, seeking union with it. Filled with desire, she becomes disoriented and sees another light; she descends toward this light, which is actually away from the light to which she was originally attracted. She descends through the earth to the realm of chaos, to the reflected light rather than to the original light, and thus finds herself in exile, in prison. There she fashions the four elements of Earth, Water, Fire and Air, and there also reside a number of beings such as the Demiurge who watches over an impressive material world now fashioned by a lion-faced being filled with the will for power. This world is characterized by outer appearance only; world as a vast source of resources to be used up in creating more power, a world devoid of the quality of soul. Sophia has to watch this happening and vows she will never abandon the world. The events of the myth indicate that Sophia is saved from the realm of chaos and ascends again to the heavens. But never forgetting her vow to be faithful to the material world, she divides herself into two beings. Heavenly Sophia is the Mary of Christian myth. She is also similar, I suspect, to the Great Goddess pursued by modern feminists, all powerful and all wise. This is not, however, the figure of our interest. Rather, our desire is to remain with the Sophia in exile; seeking connection with her adds depth and image to the material world. Thus we seek not redemption and ascension but the location of her presence within the world, even where depth seems most unlikely.

A second source of images of Sophia is the biblical tradition. Solomon the Wise speaks of Sophia in Proverbs 8. 22–29:

> The Lord knew me at the beginning of his ways; before he created anything. I was installed from eternity, from the beginning before the earth. When the deeps were not yet in existence, I was already born; when the springs were not flowing with water, before the mountains were set upon their foundations, before the hills, I was born, when he had not yet made the earth and what is upon it, nor the mountains of the surface of the earth, when he prepared the heavens, I was there. I was there when he

measured the deep, when he fixed the clouds above,
when he made firm the springs of the deep, when he set
a limit to the sea and the waters so that they should not
overstep his command, when he laid the foundation of
the earth.

This image expresses the range of the activities of
Sophia. Because she was present at the origin of the world,
Sophia is the archetypal figure of all sectors of existence.
We could travel the world seeking her manifestations and
she would never be exhausted, such is the extent of her
depth. We find her working within the world domains that
serve as backdrops for the individual letters that follow; but
our intention is to stimulate making connections with her
to the point at which a new world is discovered through the
remembering of her everywhere, in all domains.

Paracelsus provides the greatest myth of world creation
by Sophia in his "Philosophy Addressed to the Athenians."
"The Great Mystery is the mother of all," he says, and by
"Great Mystery" he means Sophia. Paracelsus compares
Sophia, in her creating power, to the artistic material that is
able to shape itself, that is at the same time the artist.
However, the comparison has a special quality, for when
one carves a sculpture from a block of wood, the shavings
are discarded; but in the shaping of the Great Mystery, the
fragments too are creative aspects of Sophia, though they
are of different qualities than the first matter. In the great
separation of the whole, there go forth first the separate
elements — Fire, Air, Water, Earth. In this myth the
elements are all of an interior nature; Paracelsus speaks of
the elements as chests, or containers — Fire as the chest of
the heavens, Air the chest of the invisible Fates, Water that
of the nymphs and sea monsters, Earth that of all growing
things, including metals. Then another separation occurs.
From the Fire are separated the stars and the planets; from
Air, the fates, impressions, incantations, superstitions, evil
deeds, dreams, visions, apparitions, spirits, and other beings
of this sort; from Water, the fish, fleshy forms, marine

monsters, nymphs, sirens; and from Earth, wood, minerals, metals, gems, fruits, flowers, herbs, seeds, animals. Here in this creation myth is presented a magnificent world as a work of art. All that we today call psychological phenomena, and in so doing subjectivize by removing from the outer world and placing in the interior of the individual or collective psyche — all are world phenomena, world beings, multiple manifestations of Sophia. In this myth we have the beginning of a psychology of the outer world, which everywhere carries an inner sense.

All that this myth says can be found in a condensed image, the World card of the Tarot. In the center of this card dances a woman with a transparent scarf thrown lightly over her shoulder and a wand in her left hand. She is surrounded by a circle of garland, and in the four corners of the card one sees an angel and an eagle above, a lion and a bull below. We are shown an image of the world as a dancing woman — not a mechanism or an organism; she is engaged in a creative act of movement and rhythm, a flowering sustained by the four elements. The scarf, lightly worn, draws aside the veil of appearance to communicate the secret essence of the soul of the world, the dance of creation.

A third source of images is found in the legend of Parzival and the search for the Grail. In the Grail stories, particularly that of Wolfram von Eschenbach, I find the women figures more significant than the heroic exploits of Parzival. Eschenbach's story tells us of Herzeloyde, Parzival's mother, abandoned by her son. It tells us of Jeschute, whom innocent Parzival gets into a great deal of trouble by taking her ring and broach; as a result of this action Jeschute is abandoned by her husband, all her belongings are taken away, and she is sent to roam the world in rags. Then there is Sigune, a virgin bride, who Parzival comes upon in the forest; she sits holding her dead husband in her lap, the original Pieta, waiting in silence. All of these women form repetitive images of Sophia — mother, lover, bride of the world. Poor dumb Parzival must gradually come to consciousness that the renewal of the world does not consist in the finding of the grail, but in developing the capacity to see the grail women who are ever present, ever faithful to the world itself. This story informs us that the point of seeking the soul of the world is in the seeking, in paying attention to what is abandoned.

Can you hold and feel these images? Sophia usually is connected with nature as the creating activity within the world. But that connection does not take us far and it takes us in the wrong direction. In past times the material world was equated with the world of nature, but that certainly is no longer the case. We now have to include all the products that humanity has brought into the world. So, if we now turn to nature to find Sophia, it is not in order to turn away from the present world but in order to gain clues concerning her modes of appearance.

When the ancient seers looked upon the world, what did they see? They saw magic. One can still see that today if one knows how to look. The seer might be walking in a forest and see among all the trees a birch — because the birch is such a conspicuous tree. It is unbelievably supple. With her beautiful white trunk she stands, yielding to the slightest movement of air, swaying amongst the more woody and unbending trees such as the oaks and beeches. No matter how old a big birch becomes, the suppleness is retained. And she does not allow herself to be overgrown. Drawing up enormous amounts of water through her roots, the birch effectively drains the ground. The seer sees these qualities and thus sees the gifts of the birch. She is wonderful medicine; since she is able to keep at bay all hardening tendencies, the birch can assist in keeping body tissues soft and supple. Because the birch drains as well she offers an effective diuretic. But we need not conclude from this example that the way to Sophia is the return to nature. It is not so much the birch that is important as it is the way of seeing the birch, seeing the magic in the birch, its soul qualities. Magic, then, is the soul of the world creating itself, according to its own laws. In the language of Goethe, magic is an urphenomenon, an irreducible reality — it cannot be analyzed into anything more basic. For Goethe, light is an urphenomenon; so is magnetism. It is not possible to reduce these phenomena to parts, not even with modern electromagnetic theory, which far from accounting for their presence, rather provides abstractions that bring the unknown under control precisely by obscuring the soul of the phenomena. It is likewise not possible to explain magic, though there are plenty of technicians of magic around. Magic is the urphenomenon of Sophia.

Now, there is magic and there is the magic of the soul of the world. Christopher Marlowe's *Faust* presents the archetypal image of individual magic, the usurpation of the realm of the magic of the world by the need for control. Faust reveals an image of elitism, of one who sought special privileges for himself and the means to obtain them. Magic here becomes the way to power, to accomplishment without responsibility, the degradation of soul wisdom to individual omnipotence. With Faust, the realm of imagination is reduced to material, outer fact, where the magician himself is the source of the magical operation. Faust, in fact, has a vision in which he sees the formation of the modern, technical world. Sophia magic, on the contrary, signifies the power of the invisible, the power of soul waiting to be released in the world. The presence of Sophia in the world offers not the artificial reshaping of the earth, but the ever present possibility of the formation of a soul consciousness in conjunction with the soul of the world.

The magical tradition, when not corrupted, never concerns an interest in personal power, but rather the passage through three gateways leading to the capacity for perception of the world soul. The first gateway concerns remembering the ancestors, passing into living relation with the ancestors. The second gateway concerns passing into a living relation with archetypal beings, and the third gateway gives passage into the soul substance of the land. Rather than coming to personal power, through these activities humans become mediators between the ancestral and archetypal beings and the archetypal substance of the land. Earth here — the land — does not carry the connotation of nature or of inert matter. The physical being of the planet is composed from numerous worlds that in the magical tradition are called the inner worlds. The inner worlds are not worlds within our imagination, but are imaginal worlds, populated by the composing beings of the fabric of the physical planet. Our imagination is the organ by which we know these composing beings. The magical world, the inner world, the psychic world is this world of the physical planet and none other. The magical tradition sustains the feeling we all have but never acknowledge, that everything is animated. Such feeling is not animism, for animism is a theory that says soul life is projected onto an inanimate world from within the human psyche. On the contrary, soul inheres within the world and creates our psyches.

What happens when we enter into the inner sense of the world? We leave the world of space and enter into the world of movement; the noun world is transformed into verb. In taking the inner sense of the world as if it were spatial rather than in motion, we are under the influence of Faust; for that is the deception of Faust, the desire to make the magical world conform to the spatial world. We see it every day — the desire to visit other places literalized into space travel; the desire to directly see other places satisfied by television; the desire to possess other worlds literalized into economics. These new literalizations are now where Sophia can be found in exile. Degradation of magic comes about with the desire for personal gain from the magical worlds. The greatest magical gifts are not powers such as seership or the attainment of wealth, but the gift of speech, active speech that does not capture but keeps the soul in active motion. Goethe for one understood this gift, not only in his poetic talent but also in his science, which is the science of the world in movement, of the soul of the world. Look to his studies of color as the metamorphosis of light and darkness, to his studies of plants and the movement of the archetypal plant, and as well his research into the metamorphosis of animals, of weather, and of geologic formations. Goethe's crowning achievement concerns the metamorphosis of the human being, the subject of his Faust, the orientation toward the return to the soul of the world.

The tradition of Sophia as the world in magic is the subject of the third card of the major arcana of the Tarot, the Empress. The Empress of the Marseille deck is pictured sitting on a throne with a back that appears like the frozen wings of an angel. She wears a two-tiered crown. In her right arm, resting on her leg, she holds a shield; the emblem on the shield is a golden eagle in flight. In her left hand she holds a scepter. The scepter consists of a long staff, sur- mounted with a globe divided horizontally in half by a belt, giving the appearance of two cups, one upside down on top of the other. The top of the globe bears a cross. She wears a blue cloak covering a red dress. A band of yellow lies as a necklace, and directly below she wears a belt of gold over the blue cloak.

The two levels of the crown of the Empress indicate her authority over two planes; she serves that which is above and that which is below. The crown further indicates a consciousness of her position, that is, she possesses con- scious understanding of the world. The golden eagle in flight images the world as a world of movement, its soul life as rhythm and motion. The scepter depicts that through which the action of magic occurs. The bottom half of the globe surmounting this scepter shows the power of recep- tivity. The top half of the globe shows the influx of soul into the world. The cross on top of the globe images the perfect union of receptive power with soul, the unity of the vertical and the horizontal world, of depth spread through- out the physical world. The red and blue of the dress signify the world as vital and alive, through the circulation of the blood of soul, and the golden necklace and belt signify the yoking of soul and world. In this magnificent figure of the Tarot we have an image of Sophia that provides all we need for beginning the work of seeing through the outer world to its inner essence.

In introducing Sophia as Empress of the Tarot, the figure of sacred magic, we must not lose our connection with the world by taking this image as belonging to a spiritual discipline having nothing to do with the daily outside world. Sophia is then abandoned and we are off on a spiritual or psychological trip concerned only with personal development. All the while we miss the significance of the image, to bring the world into psychological work. There exists, however, one phenomenon with which we are all familiar, even if we have no knowledge of occult traditions, that presents a prime image of magic as the soul of the world. It is a phenomenon that exists in the world but at the same time disappears unless given attention. This phenomenon is the rainbow. We all feel the appearance of a rainbow as a magical event. The rainbow unites the above and the below, and the outcome of this bridging is color. When we behold the rainbow we are not looking at nature merely in an outer aspect; we are face to face with, we are directly perceiving the soul of the world. The rainbow is at the same time the only phenomenon in nature that depends for its appearance not only on sun and earth but also on us, for the rainbow itself moves with the observer. Each person sees his own separate bow of color, and yet that color belongs to the world. The rainbow was venerated by the Egyptians under the name of Isis, that is to say, Sophia. The rainbow is a rare appearance of the archetype that nonetheless works throughout the outer world, a phenomenon of pure movement that gives the world its color. That the rainbow does not appear except through attention given to it indicates that Sophia waits; magic needs the agreement of the human in order to show forth.

What are the terms of the agreement? What must be done to enliven the resonance between ourselves and the soul of the world? Here I wish to give a few indications of the kind of practice involved in the development of these letters. The primary practice is silence, the first aspect of magic. Through silence we are able to approach the creating powers of the soul of the world. These powers are qualitative experiences of the world in which there is no separation between what is purely physical and what is purely of the soul element. The tradition names these creating powers Earth, Air, Fire, and Water. Everything of this world is created through the transformation of these elements that are the active powers of the soul of the world. Four other arts accompany the entrance into silence — concentration, meditation, picture-making, and contemplation. With concentration we enter into the creating powers of Air; concentration is the uniting with the Air element. With meditation we enter into the creating powers of Fire, the capacity of thinking so intensely that the fire within things illuminates them from within. With picture-making we enter into the creating powers of Water; that is, imagination is the Water element, perfectly reflecting the inner essence of the outer world. With contemplation we enter into the creating powers of elemental earth; contemplation — to move within the temple of the soul of the world. Seen through Sophia, the so-called spiritual disciplines become a way of facing the world with soul.

We are accustomed to taking concentration, meditation, picture-making (or imaging), and contemplation as belonging to individual consciousness when they are, it seems to me, a giving over of individual consciousness to the consciousness that is the soul of the world. Concentration is the art of forgetting our own subjectivity in order to be fully available to what presents itself. When the activities of personal thinking and personal feeling are stilled, the subjectivity of the outer world expresses itself. Meditation is a new kind of thinking, not going off to an ashram or a private room to ah and om, but leaving behind the physical brain, which can only reflect the material world in its outer aspect, in order to enter into the intelligence of things. Thus, meditation is the intensification of intelligence, the warmth and light within things. Picture-making or imaging unfolds from the action of meditation. Images are reflections of the warmth of meditation, they are a reflective intelligence. But this intelligence must maintain intimate connection with concentration and meditation; alone, imaging focuses only on the product and picturing becomes looking at pictures. And then contemplation — the call to contemplative life no longer implies removal from the world, but the exact opposite, constant mobile relation with the movement of the soul of the world.

In the following letters these arts of the soul constitute the practice that fosters the attempt to move into the consciousness soul to achieve the fully conscious presence of the soul of the world. As you shall see, I have eschewed methods that would most easily evoke this kind of presence of the world in order to avoid nostalgic primitivism, a view of the world of nature as better than the actual world with which we must daily contend, and above all to avoid the development of purely personal abilities and powers.

Return now to the opening question — who is Sophia? An answer that condenses everything I have said thus far, a final image of Sophia, can be found in the *Golden Ass* of Apuleius. After his many travails and after having been turned into an ass, Lucius in this novel, which occurs at the time of the disappearance of the creating powers of the universe and the coming into dominance of the human intellect, is in a desperate place and turns to implore Sophia for help. He then falls asleep, and she appears in a dream. Here is the dream image:

> First, she had an abundance of hair that fell gently in dispersed ringlets upon her neck. A crown of interlaced wreaths and varying flowers rested upon her head; and in its midst, just over the brow, there hung a plain circlet resembling a mirror or rather a miniature moon — for it emitted a soft clear light. This ornament was supported on either side by vipers that rose from the furrows of the earth; and above it blades of corn were disposed. Her garment, dyed many colors, was woven of fine flax. One

part was gleaming white; another was yellow as the crocus; another was flamboyant with the red of roses. But what obsessed my gazing eyes by far the most was her pitch-black cloak that shone with a dark glow. It was wrapped round her, passing from under the right arm over the left shoulder and fastened with a knot like the boss of a shield. Part of it fell down in pleated folds and swayed gracefully with a knotted fringe along the hem. Upon the embroidered edges and over the whole surface sprinkled stars were burning; and in the center a mid-month moon breathed forth her floating beams. Lastly a garland wholly composed of every kind of fruit and flower clung of its own accord to the flutter border of that splendid robe.

Then Sophia speaks to Lucius, and we hear from her who she is:

Behold Lucius, moved by your prayer I come to you — I, the natural mother of all life, the mistress of the elements, the first child of time, the supreme divinity, the queen of those below, the first among those in heaven, the uniform manifestation of all the gods and goddesses — I who govern by my nod the crests of light in the sky, the purifying wafts of the ocean, and silences of below.

Sophia, rhythmic dance of the soul of the world, rainbow of colors and forms, you are the world as a work of art, and you demand from us to understand the world artistically rather than intellectually. But at the same time, art need not be separated from intellect, imagination need not be removed from thought. The formation of a consciousness that can hold these capacities together seems to me to be the task of this age, and a further part of that task involves the development of the capacity to center such imaginal thought within the events of the world as we now face them. Active imaginal thought promotes the gradual transforming of the taken for granted notion that it is we who are doing the thinking to the stance that it is the world that thinks through us.

If intellectual thought and abstraction constitute the source of the all-pervading world malaise, it is not thought itself that is the disease but the fact that thinking is in need of living qualities. We approach the world as if it is already finished, completed, and we approach consciousness as if it is also already finished. When one thinks in the ordinary way, for example, one is aware of the object of thought but not of the activity of thought itself. This disease of consciousness is now universal, as pointed out by Georg Kuhlewind, and is the disease of thinking with dead thoughts, thoughts that have already been thought, forms that are already complete. And if one attempts to avoid this disease by turning instead to image, the situation is no different — I am aware of the picture, but not of the picturing. And then if one instead turns to feeling, the situation is even worse. With thought it is at least possible to be aware that one is aware of the thought but not the thinking. Feeling does not even have this limited autonomy. We are moved by feelings, suffer them, and once there they have their way with us. I can think what I choose to, but I cannot choose to feel a given feeling at will. In all realms of consciousness we are aware of the content of consciousness but not of the act itself because the act is a world act that we have come to take as our own, thereby producing an impenetrable veil over the world.

The only way to lift this veil is to think on the side of the world. One makes an effort to think in step with the thought of the world; thus it becomes necessary to approach the given world, not the world as one would like it to be. The next step is to try to be attentive with a deeper level of the soul, to perceive the feelings of the world through one's feeling of the world. This requires total silence on the part of all feelings of attraction or repulsion. It is not a question of the feelings that the world calls up in me, but of the feelings through which I feel the world, just as a work of art can be experienced through its own feeling.

Then, in the expression of the world as it thinks itself through one, one tries to make sure not to say anything superfluous, to speak only when there is something there that speaks. There follows the attempt to become one with the world occurrence, the occurrence of a world which seems at first formally understandable, but whose soul remains hidden. What is now spoken, thought, imaged, does not have the aim of being informative, but presents itself in soul in order to be realized. This kind of imaginal thought does not have as its aim a flash of understanding after which we fall back into an experience of "now I have it." The aim is a real dwelling in the element from which we normally only register flashes, and those only after they are over and done with.

What is the aim of approaching the world in this manner? The aim is not only to realize the soul in the world but also to make the soul of the world, to increase the giving out of soul in order to make soul. In order to make this aspect of the work clear I must return to the previous image of the Tarot World card. In describing this image I omitted a significant detail. I stated that the dancing woman carries a wand in her left hand, an emblem of sacred magic. In her right hand she is holding something else, a barely discernible object that can only be described as a philter, a magical potion or charm, an emblem of illusory magic. Through this aspect of the image we must confront the power of illusion when focusing on the world. The manner of approaching soul in the world I have described in terms of the wand, of magic, and world as magic. We are now in the midst of a time when there appears to be very strong concern for the world — for ecology, preservation, restoration, control of pollution, recycling, saving the animals, saving the forests, curbing corporations, saving the planet. The world is very much on our minds. *All of these actions are not on the side of the wand but on the side of the magic potion, on the side of illusion, because they all assume that it is we who can gain control through enacting measures of restraint on destructive forms of consciousness; they do not propose a radical alteration of consciousness itself.* Alone, these measures encourage the illusion that with carefulness and planning we can be in charge of the world, treat her better than our immediate predecessors. However, we are not lords of the planet. An alloying of the truth that we are ourselves an aspect of the world with the falsehood that we are in charge produces illusion. One might think that in this day and age each of us has plenty to worry about — pollution, devastation of land and forests, acid rain, overdevelopment; now we are told that in addition, we have to worry about our consciousness. If by some great act all the problems of ecology, for example, were politically solved tomorrow, within less than a month all these same problems would be back. For the real problem is diseased consciousness. We can throw money, programs, policies endlessly into these world concerns and absolutely nothing will be different. The aim of the approach in these letters is not the solution of problems but the making of soul.

These letters do not progress like logical thought. Moving from one letter to another is more like following a mosaic — or perhaps the letters lack even that sense of order. If the reader comes to this work in a conventional state of awareness, confusion may result, producing marked discomfort. And the discomfort may be further enhanced by the fact that when one comes to psychology there is the expectation that the human being will be at the center (we are always fascinated with ourselves). Thus, dear friend, prepare to be disturbed, though my intention is not to seek disturbance for its own sake. This unfortunate effect of the work will, I hope, stimulate soul capacities that have slumbered long in the history of humanity. You may feel an initial hopelessness as you enter into the faces of the world that I present; but that feeling too belongs to Sophia, that feeling of being in exile while nonetheless within the midst of everything of the world.

This work may also engender the fearful experience that the literal world, the world that we all rely on in order to get up every day and function is dissolving. Psychology as presently known and practiced works precisely because one feels the safety of the conception of the world as a literal place, an ever-present solid background enabling one to leave for a time to go on internal trips where everything has a dreamlike quality of constant motion. We are most willing to go on psychological trips of one sort or another, confident that we can return to the illusion of a world of concrete stability. With the approach to the soul of the world that follows, that illusion is taken away, as the work of centuries to produce a world of maya is exposed.

It is now commonplace to say that the only stability is change, and in the midst of living in an illusion of stability that now seems to shift frequently, though periodically, the cliche of change is comforting because it does not make much of a demand. This dictum merely states that one must be prepared, for tomorrow the world will be different. It does not compel living in change as the constant of the present. Nor does it speak to the necessity of forming the capacity to experience change as an activity instead of as only a product. Thus, we are able to sustain the illusion of a stable literal world, allaying the anxiety that the world may be different tomorrow with the confidence that it will be possible to make the adjustment.

This work on the soul of the world narrows the gap between the reliable and the unknown and dislodges the feeling that no matter what, control will be possible. The question arises: if it becomes possible to accept that Sophia is behind all this change in the world, and that inviting her out of exile seems to be accompanied by such uncomfortable results, is it not better to keep her confined? In the last letter I will attempt to respond to this pressing question. Here I only indicate that Sophia is accompanied by an archetypal helpmate. This soul mate does not offer stability but functions as one through whom it becomes possible to enjoy instability and navigate in it, though not to control it. This helpmate is even more occluded than Sophia. I must allow her to speak first.

LETTER II

House and City

DEAR FRIEND,

The intention of these letters is to suggest ways the forces
of the soul can regenerate the outer world. Let us begin
with the physical structures within which daily life takes
place, our home and our city. A building is not an object
when seen through the powers of the soul, but a being
whose subjectivity has been suppressed. The symptoms
include feelings of isolation, loss of speech, absence of
relation with others, loss of memory, an anorectic body,
superficial glitter, and vacuous inner life. As we let the
houses, office towers, public buildings, malls make an
impression on us, such feelings arise, not as what we feel
about them, but as the manner in which they express
themselves. The prototype for such suffering by buildings is
the glittering, glassy tower set down upon the earth as if
from above, closed in on itself, unrelated to the landscape
as a whole, dedicated to the gods of productivity. Deprived
of language, showing forth no interesting detail, modern
buildings suffer unbearable monotony. The structure of the
modern world found perfect expression in Le Corbusier. He
delighted in altering architecture from the expression of the
soul of the world to a manifestation of egotism. He said:
"Our youthful friends did not know what Art is — deep
love of one's ego, which one seeks in retreat and solitude,
this divine ego which can be terrestrial ego when it is forced
by struggle to become so." When architecture becomes
"egotecture" we live and work in inflated, hollow, monoto-
nous, self-reliant, lonely, flashy, defiant space. Seeing

through these defenses, through the reflective glass and the thin facade, we discover that such places cry to be clothed with soul. You might feel that the house provides the needed soul place where rhythmic regeneration takes place, but houses now lack the same psychological roots in the continuity of the past as do the skeletal productions of the city. An endless housing development is no more than a skyscraper laid out in the horizontal, just as a tower is no more than that same monotony stacked vertically.

A quite remarkable contemporary artist, Christo, provides a way to begin clothing the built environment with soul. His art consists of wrapping landscapes and structures with cloth. Several years ago he wrapped the entire Pont Neuf Bridge in Paris, a labor of ten years preparation, which when completed lasted but several weeks. What is he doing, wrapping the things of the world? It is as if the life of this bridge, its animation, had sunk deep into the matter; few felt its soul anymore. Healing the bridge, for Christo, does not involve physical renovation or updating, but restoring its subtle imagination. This art touches things again without harming them. It puts us in touch with substantial reality, it uses things without using them up, it regenerates their souls. That Christo turns to existing physical objects while so much contemporary art emphasizes abstract forms, colors, feelings, or inner psychic images makes his work an aberration of importance. He sees something that no one else dares to face; the physical world, the body of imagination, the world's body has entered a state of almost irretrievable numbness. No healing will be found for this illness that will not entail a reversal of our way of imagining the world, placing it first and ourselves second. If we learn to enter these sufferings of the world more imaginatively, if we take them to heart with a vision that can sense the subtle exchange ever possible between the individual soul and the world soul, new forces can enter the outer world. "The silent world," says Francis Ponge, poet of things, "is our only homeland." Of all we see, hear, feel, and touch, the substance is and must be in ourselves; and therefore there is no alternative between the dreary belief that everything in the world being dead, we are the living dead and the belief that the soul that is in us is in the things of the world likewise. The basic error of our entire present-day conception of the world lies in thinking that spirit and soul make their appearance outside the physical world.

The long historical process of materializing the world has led to the outlook of facing a dead world. This process concerns freeing consciousness from participation with the things of the world, resulting in control over them. A crucial and very subtle aspect of this freedom, however, concerns the development of the soul capacity to freely and consciously engage the world. We achieve this soul capacity by encouraging imagination to cohere with thinking.

Imagination serves as homeopathic elixir that heals; the practice of such healing requires that one experience the soul of the outer world through one's inner eye of soul. Attending to such imaginative vision does not require us to become mystics or to take the inward journey but rather to give attention to the world. I view the history of depth psychology as a preparatory discipline whose task remains incomplete as long as it concentrates solely on the individual psyche. Archetypal psychology constitutes an advance of Jung's psychology by focusing on image not as something to be seen, but as something to "see through." The "seeing through" is related to archetypal figures — gods, goddesses, spirits, angels, daemons — a whole imaginal world that creates soul. "Seeing through" can be taken a step further when we ask, "What do the figures of the imaginal world see?" They see imaginally, mythically, their seeing leads to a mythologizing of the world.

Let us begin with the house, because it being the place where we awake every morning it provides the most immediate opportunity for awakening soul to the outer world. It does not matter if you live in an apartment or condominium rather than a house; the image of the house evokes archetypal, permanent aspects of earth connected with the desire to feel at home in the world. The house is more than a box within which to live; it is a soul activity to be retrieved from the numbness of the world of modern objects. Each place of the house, each room, hallway, closet, stair, and alcove is a distinct structure that animates different aspects of soul. Without such differences, eating, sleeping, making love, sitting, bathing, even talking become merely biological activities. And these activities revert to the biological when soul does not wrap the impoverished dwelling. The particular soul qualities with which I wish to clothe the neglected house are the imagination of doors, windows, and rooms.

For a psychology taking its stance on the side of the world, doors have soul. They are guardians of boundaries, they serve both to divide and to connect the psychic topography of the house, keeping its imagination multiple, and each part in direct or indirect relation with every other part. Doors make and mark tension between the diverse elements within the house. The most complex door is the entrance, for it must bear the greatest tension — keeping the inside secure without barring entry completely, signaling the individuality of this house while appearing commonplace. The importance accorded the entrance shows in the ornamentation framing it. Where such framing is absent, the patterning or figuration on the door itself announces the necessity of hesitancy, of a moment of purification and initiation before entering into a sacred body. The art of the door makes of arriving, departing and returning a ritual process that assures that the house will not be taken for granted. Clothe your entrance with such images.

Doors possess magical qualities in stories, fairy tales, and folklore. They are the entrances and exits through which imagination moves. It is possible to live in one room; many do so, but those who live in a single room create many invisible doors. Doors introduce time and rhythm into the house, acting as punctuation marks, slowing the restless urge for movement into pauses. Certain kinds of doors suffer in the extreme and need particular soul care. Metal doors are absolute barriers, which are primarily defenses. Hollow doors make the house empty, no matter how much it has in it or how many people. Sliding glass doors are cruel — Louis Kahn calls them "hair-raising, brutal, like a guillotine." And the door without careful framing is equally cruel. It may have severe metal bands that make passing through more like entering a compression chamber than like changing psychic space; or, it may have no frame and confuse us with its lack of circumspection.

* * *

Things appear in the invisible intermediary of windows as they do through imagination itself. We do not just see out of windows, we see through them. The house not only receives light through the window, it becomes an interior place through the medium of glass. The glass turns the subtlety of psychic reflection inward. We are drawn to staring through windows, as if in a dream state induced by this medium.

Windows allow the house its dreams. They make the house psychic, interior space. Without imagination, windows are no more than holes in the wall. When there are smaller panes rather than sheets of glass, house and window are intimately intermingled. Then the window does not forget that it belongs to the house and that it is the servant of the house's soul. Larger windows do something different. They make the house self-conscious, more open and vulnerable, more unsure. Large picture windows change seeing through into looking at and being seen, instilling paranoia in the house. It is as if the inside did not wish to be exhibited or displayed, its veil of mystery removed. At night when lighted from within the house is betrayed by the large window. Are passersby not embarrassed to be so privy to the inner life of the house? But the inner glow of light through small windows, on the contrary, lets those who pass by sense the inner warmth of an interior life.

The room without a window is the prison cell of the house. Such rooms reflect only individual personality, as if the house did not matter. Prisons lack windows for exactly this reason. They are places without dreams. The criminal becomes a criminal to himself when faced with his own image on every wall; the object of the architecture of the prison is to impress upon the criminal who he is: to appeal to his conscience to seek forgiveness.

We would feel suffocated without windows; windows give breath to the house. With breath comes rhythm and a different interiority than empty space which is static because it cannot experience the constant exchange of inside and outside.

* * *

Although there are specific features to each room of the house, the soul of the room rests in the conversations it sets up with things. The multiplication of rooms reveals multiple dimensions of soul, or depth. The animation of the bedroom, for example, shows through the things of the bed, the chest of drawers, the carefully arranged lamps, mirrors, bedspread, vanity. The same with each room. Things detail the image, making it particular. But things are alive when they are able to express themselves in multiple ways. A bed is not a living room. But the bedroom is not alive when the bed is only for sleeping or making love. Ladies of the eighteenth century reclined in bed to receive guests. And does not the bed make a good reading room, bringing out the dream quality of books? For the child the bed is a playground. The bed can also be a quiet corner in which to pray or an intimate breakfast table. Matisse sculpted in bed.

Each room contains a mythic universe. The bedroom, dreamroom of the house, becomes awake when we sleep and fills with ancestors, daemons, animals, unspeakable acts, unknown creatures, and other fears not admitted to

conscious life. The kitchen, an alchemical laboratory filled
with vessels, powders, mixing instruments, delicious and
repugnant smells, works on the transformation of fantasy
into flesh. The living room weaves the random strands of
daily living into conversation, brings them to focus before
the hearth. The dining room bridges the activities of the
kitchen and the living room. The bathroom was not incor-
porated into the house until the nineteenth century. The
first indoor baths were installed in a New Jersey hotel in
1853, a half century before the bathroom entered the house.
Such an origin connects the bath of the house with the
image of luxury, comfort, and convenience. At the same
time the bathroom is connected with images of medical
treatment. The sanitary enamel fixtures as well as the
shower were early medical instrumentation for the treatment of gout and abdominal maladies. The bath also
belongs to the cosmos of Venus — sweet smells, fine oils,
sensuous powders, vanity. And nature abides here with
soaps smelling of pine, sweet flowers, dew drops. Adding
the toilet to the bath is relatively recent and dulls the
archetypal memory of bathing as a communal ritual that
had as its purpose, not the washing away of dirt, but the
regeneration of body and soul. But one ought not forget the
sheer pleasure of elimination, a small act that preserves the
soul of the bathroom.

The alchemists practiced certain disciplines to engage
imagination with the things of the world. John Lash tells of
how a discipline of concentration was central to their work.
We can apply such practices in the laboratory of the world.
Imagine a particular house. To form such an image requires
an act of concentration. The more detail and the more exact
the detail, the more concentration is required. The house
appears at the point of attention. But where is this point of
attention? All we can say is that the image of the house is
free-floating, unlocatable.

Now, look at an actual house and do something odd
—interpenetrate the image of the house with the materiality of the house. This second act of concentration produces

a distinct sensation of release, an easing of attention, a subtle but unmistakable impression. The feeling of release of inner attention produced by this act was common in the work of the alchemists and known as "extraction." The image does live in the materiality, but in the "massa confusa," the beginning of the alchemical work of transforming thing into soul. The process of ensouling the world follows this kind of discipline. For example, the house is not only a thing but also consciousness of the essence of the thing. Through becoming conscious, it becomes. Imagining the house is the house becoming conscious. Through such an alchemical work the house lives.

* * *

The city houses the communal soul. Restoring the city means restoring its soul, wrapping the city daily with the act of imagination. The city can no longer be limited to distinct places, for the imagination of city now encompasses the world completely, even if one lives on a farm or spends time in the wilderness. Renewal of soul can no longer rest on a fantasy of returning to nature; renewal rests on returning to the nature of soul. Now nature too is a psychological construction; it did not exist until the advent of the modern city. Now that city is all pervasive we need not hold on to nature; instead we must relate city to earth. The city is our home, but the earth is our dwelling place. We live on the earth, beneath the sky, the drifting clouds and the stars, and the golden sun. The sun lights our world and gives warmth and measures the course of day; the glow of moon bathes the night and its changing cycles form the rhythms of the ocean and growing plants. The weather forms the seasons. The play of all of these elements differs according to where we are on the earth, so that a city is not just anywhere, it is a particular locus of the earth elements, an expressive play of those elements that are the forming forces of its soul.

The first act of imagination required to regenerate the

soul of the city is the locating of the image within actual places of the world. Imagination congeals into the city — a complete imaginal, mythical world that grounds, sustains, and enlivens the soul, clothing it with a habitation and a name. But the city, seen through soul, is a gathering together of elemental beings of the world soul into a particular landscape in order to be brought further into the workings of the world — as city.

Landscape becomes art when shaped into the architecture of the city. When cities begin to all appear the same it is because earth has been forgotten. The concern with planetary ecology represents a similar forgetfulness of the particularity of place, requiring a disembodied caring that leads to abstract programs and ideologies. Better to awake each morning with the small exercise of remembering that you are here, not everywhere. The ensouling of city then becomes an individual task, a daily exercise that strengthens the powers of soul. Better city planning will not alter anything because such planning takes place in a technical world. (In Letter VI I examine the particular challenges to the soul presented by technology.) I suggest that each individual open the door to the world, travel through the thickness of the things of the city, seeing them through image. How can we possibly say what might be good for a city when we have only to focus attention on the first object in sight to find that no one has ever really looked from its point of view. If we are to speak of the city we must become unconscious of ourselves and take the side of the soul of the city.

Since the mid 1940s, technology, not as mechanism but as medium, has swept over the planet like a giant windstorm completely reshaping the conditions of the world. It has produced global urbanization as the primary mode of life, with the skyscraper its architectural symbol. The skyscraper condenses and makes visible the conditions of technological life. The skyscraper dominates the actual city; it now dominates the architecture of the soul as well, and at great price, for we do not know how to live with a form which by design excludes the participation of the soul. At the same time, the tremendous power of this mode of world manifestation makes it impossible to simply turn back to architectural symbols with soul — to the circle, the cave, the hut, the maze, the spiral, the village.

The built environment of the technical world prohibits the spontaneous experience of soul. Skyscrapers may be spectacular, dazzling, powerful, but they are also numbing, anesthetic. These buildings take control of life through their capacity to dull the subtlety of soul. Part of the practice of finding soul again involves experiencing rage in the face of such control, but it also involves experiencing compassion for those buildings — for they are ill. The clean sharp lines of glass-box buildings, the orderly layouts of city streets, cubical offices, and boxy-tunneled corridors introduce the sickness of normality into the city. The norm is the square — right angle means right action — decisive, clear, clean, moral, sharp, immediate, without reflection. Right-angled mentality encourages expansion without limits because the straight line, if it stops expanding, dies. Our work is to look upon all this, our actual situation, and bring in the complexity of soul.

* * *

A psychotherapy patient tells a dream: it is a dream of walking with a beautiful woman in a California courtyard, under a veranda surrounded with greenery and flowers. The dreamer does not know this woman from waking life. They walk, hand in hand, and sit quietly together, looking into each others eyes. They kiss. The alarm goes off. He has to get up, get the children ready for school, fix breakfast, shower, put the dog out, and get ready to go into the city. He curses, angry and frustrated, wishing the dream would have come to a conclusion before his having to face the world. He wishes he had more time for his own inner life. I suggest to him that the soul arranged the dream in exactly the manner needed. The dream is not about his "inner woman." The dream shows him there exists a radical break between soul and city. Imagination for him is lovely, inner, sensual, and private. Rather than wanting this all for himself, he could be helped by the dream to clothe the day with erotic beauty; the dream might inspire not love for his inner woman but imagination with which to wrap the city that day. If he cannot feel that, he will either want to chuck it all and run off to California or to cultivate his inner life, hoping the suffering city will be handled by the politicians, the developers, and the planners. What might the city be like if we awoke, grateful for the gift of a dream, a fragment of imagination through which to face the city? And what of ugly or frightening dreams, or weird pathological ones? City encompasses all.

Bringing such images to the city makes us forget ourselves, makes us unselfconscious, and recenters feelings over there, merged with the things. Because technical architecture does not produce a sympathetic response of soul, soul must be given to it. This involves relinquishing the subjectivity of our inner concerns and acting as if things which we do not like mattered. In the ancient world, the organ for perception of the world was the heart. Present perception tends to be bi-located — in the head and in the genitals — with a great cavity of repressed anxiety in between. We see not what is there but what we conceptualize, and imagination collects around sex. It is the heart, however, that is simultaneously the organ of perception and the organ of imagination. The heart responds to beauty. It can also project beauty. We make a building beautiful when we stop for it, arrest the motion of thoughts, and linger with it, rather than merely using it. A glass tower is not unlike a computer. Both are media whose message is to increase efficiency. To spend time each day giving attention to a technical building where one works is a very unfamiliar gesture toward a thing designed to receive little attention, designed to focus attention on efficient work. The soul work here consists of defamiliarizing it, loosening the web of anesthesia.

Now, some suggestions on practice, on how to ensoul the city. Some of the following may seem wild and unfeasible; my intent is to spark imagination. Much can be carried on quite easily in daily life. For example, one might begin making a psychological handbook on how to live with a technical building. Partly, such a manual is diagnostic —what is the matter with the building; partly, the manual is prognostic — what one might do to care for the building with soul. Partly, the manual consists of meditations on the life of the building — its moods, what it displays and what it hides, its sensitivities, its relations to its neighbors.

Some time ago I was asked to speak to a group of city managers on the topic of architecture and the quality of life in the city. The meeting took place in a small room in the city's convention center. The room itself was sick. It had no windows, and the drab acoustic ceilings pressed in from above, sandwiching the room with oppression. The door was without a handle. It had only a steel plate for the hand and was indistinguishable from a public restroom entry. No molding marked a difference between ceiling and walls, and between walls and floor. Painted institutional gray, its floor covered with rough carpet, the space was filled with ugly brown folding chairs. The conversation in that space was interesting. It all gravitated toward power. A group of fairly ordinary people, city workers, all began talking about how they would change the architecture of the city. But no one noticed the suffering of this room. So how would it be possible to trust how they would reshape the city? The room was filled either with complaints or with cheerleader promotions of the achievements of the city. It is not surprising that in an empty space such as this the imagination of power took hold. The room was not used but used up; it felt neglected, abused, tricked. Nevertheless, a great deal could be done to care for the soul of the room, starting with the recognition that it is hurting. What could be done? Simple things. A small table with a flower placed on it would honor the room. Anything given to the room that indicates through its presence a linking between this place and the larger world honors the room by saying that it is part of the world and not a space capsule. Anything that gives sensory experience to the room retrieves the soul from abstraction. A flower, a wooden table, a ceramic vase, a little earth, the necessary watering of a plant — with such gestures we have located this room on earth. Of course, if all the rooms of this convention center were suddenly supplied with tables and plants, all that was achieved through this suggestion would be lost so long as each room was not treated according to its particularity by the particularity of an individual soul. Sensory experience is needed, but imagination must be the primary ingredient. Nothing would be further off the mark than to hire a decorating firm to come in and prettify one abstraction with an additional one.

* * *

The approach to the soul of the city I have in mind can best be carried forth by individuals, as a kind of ongoing therapy in daily life. First, we must have the felt recognition that the dominance of technical architecture and city design deadens the soul, and we must realize that the city is dying, in spite of its glitter and flash and self-promotion. Once we get through denial, a response of rage follows. It makes us want to flee the city. Rage — felt, held, not shut off nor denied nor acted out — leads to compassion. Compassion must be nurtured to the point that one suffers with things. Compassion opens the soul, an opening which can lead to a different perception of the city, one which ceases merely to look at the city and begins to engage the city's invisible soul.

In order for anything to express itself, it needs to be held in positive regard. But this regard is not a judgment of the thing as beautiful when it is not, or as good when it is not. The positive regard is the capacity to experience the particularity of the things of the world in an attitude of silence and waiting. The heart says yes there is something here to behold beyond what I think or feel about it. The heart does not strive after meaning, but rather allows the things to disclose themselves.

These suggestions are likely to be met at first with skepticism. They might appear to be of no practical value, for they do not seem to alter the actual cityscape. Such an attitude diminishes soul by assuming that it has no power. The kind of perception that stares out of a vacuous body onto a world of inanimate things is a relatively recent development — beginning about the sixteenth century, the time modern economics began to take hold. This manner of abstractly viewing the world has since shaped the world. It is a development that has allowed us to gain power over the material world, and it is the stance that makes us live in dread of holocaust, the final result of the idea of the world as dead. The holocaust began the moment the world was declared dead; all anxiety about the actual end is the accumulation of the daily dread of the destructive power over things. Give us this day our daily dread, but let us feel it.

Stress, burnout, anorexia, bulimia, drugs, heart attack, cancer — are these not the illnesses of the modern world? Do they not well up first in the outer world, and are not our sufferings merely the ways through which the silent world finds expression? Stress does not center on human beings but refers to physical matter that has been deprived of imagination, treated mechanically. Burnout can be viewed as deriving from the burnt-out world that has continued to function without inspiration. Anorexia and bulimia aptly describe the world stripped of feminine spirit. Drugs are all artificial spirits, manufactured sham replacements of the imagination of the world. Heart attack relates to the removal of beauty from the world, producing heart-stopping anxiety. With cancer we clearly see how the ensouled body of the world is taken over by an imitation body. The complaints of the thingly world are our modern diseases.

They are all here to stimulate a next phase in the evolution of soul, the return of soul to world.

The materials now employed to make the built environment lack the touch of the human hand, handcraft being the traditional mediator through which the world soul reshapes itself into images suitable for given historical circumstances. And yet, while everyone decries the shoddiness of modern materials, a return to handcraft does not appear possible. When it does occur, it tends to produce quaintness rather than soul. Even worse, when modern materials are used and buildings made in the design of times in which people imagine soul still existed in the world, one has the feeling of visiting shoddy antiques. Thus, it seems that the question of returning soul to the built environment carries a certain hopelessness. In this letter I have attempted to address the question in a different, more subtle manner; one might call what I offer suggestions on how to live in hopelessness. The dilemma does point out that now the weight of the soul tends to be on our side, over against the world, and the demand is one of developing the capacity to make strong images, to always realize that these images are not ours but the productions of the soul of the world, to whom they are to be returned. The history of the fate of imagination unreturned to the world is the story of the tragic fate of romanticism, within which I also locate the development of depth psychology. The most significant tenets of depth psychology can be found first stated by the Romantics; for example, the term "self-realization" was first put forth by Coleridge, the term "individuation" by Hopkins. And, most important, imagination forms the central notion of all romanticism.

Romanticism is a large topic. It can hardly be called a coherent movement, so varied are its representatives; but, according to John Lash, of all the varieties of approach and personalities involved, we find two things upon which all the romantics have agreed: the centrality of imagination and the presence of the divine, not out in the universe somewhere, but within. Blake goes so far as to say the resurrection body of Christ is imagination. Romanticism contains the optimism that we can become our own gods, a proposition put forth directly by Shelley. I do not wish to address this second aspect of romanticism, but the first. The romantic adventure concentrated on the development of imagination and the cultivation of the inner life. When, however, the romantics tried to live in the world through the centrality of imagination, we find romanticism turned into decadence, at around 1885. The decadents attempted to live the inner life and only the inner life, but they discovered this attempt impossibile to sustain. Consequently, they led more and more bizarre lives, separating off from the world to become the Bohemians. This tragedy, I believe, resulted from separating imagination from the world. Modern Jungian psychology tends toward a similar exhaustion. I am continually amazed at how many analysts, whose work also consists of promoting the inner life, split themselves in two. One local analyst hands out his business card, and underneath his name the card reads "Jungian analyst, Episcopal priest, and investment counselor." Soul making, it seems to me, must be world-oriented rather than self-oriented; otherwise cultivation of soul is at the expense of world. The tremendous force that comes about through the cultivation of the inner life can produce radical changes in the outer world, if it is oriented in that direction always. Just as the idea of materialism, a shadowy intellectual construction of what the world is actually like, has brought about an unimaginable world, concentration on soul of the world can bring about a world of imagination. It does not take large numbers. The romantics numbered a few hundred at the most. Who knows what might happen with the discipline of daily clothing the world with imagination.

LETTER III

Learning Through Soul

DEAR FRIEND,

Each of these letters focuses on a particular way to face the world with soul and need not be read in the order presented, for the letters do not follow a logical argument but are intended to stimulate imagination on the side of the world. I want now to speak of learning and education. The contribution of Jung to the field of education lies elsewhere than in the few writings in which he specifically discusses the psychology of child development and learning. Education is a cultural enterprise, and as the word itself says, education concerns guidance of soul into the world. A large part of Jung's psychology, what we might call the world side of his endeavor, takes historical manifestations of culture — myths, symbols, ritual, art, literature, science, medicine —and shows how all of these products are also spontaneously created by the picture consciousness of the individual soul. Further, when we read Jung, not with an academic mentality, but with a meditative consciousness, we find that the spontaneous creativity of the individual soul makes a work of art and that that work of art is the human body. Remember, for example, his observation that soul forms a continuous spectrum, a rainbow in which the blue end is consciousness and the red end instinct. In this manner Jung holds body and consciousness together as both being soul manifestations. The body that soul creates, as Jung demonstrates through uncovering the tradition in this area, is the whole cosmos in microcosmic form. It follows, then, that the display of soul in the world, brought about through the act of human making, constitutes culture. Education in this sense concerns the drawing out of soul to conjoin with world soul, and participation in culture consists of living in the unity of soul visible in the world. This is a far cry from what currently passes as education, for here education is an ongoing unfolding of soul. Education instead has become an institution whose purpose in the modern world is not to make culture, not to serve the living cosmos, but to harness humankind to the dead forces of materialism. Education as we know it, from preschool through graduate school, damages the soul.

Materialism is far more than a concern for material goods. It is an outlook that says all processes of the world, of the body, and of life can be accounted for on the basis of the combination of material processes and the laws governing their ways of combining. Materialism not only reduces the world to abstract processes, it involves the total exclusion of the working of invisible soul beings in the earthly sphere. Materialistic learning that supports this world view dominates education in the sciences, and the humanities also partake of this reduction. When myths are approached as remnants of the past, or when the cosmos is confined to the sphere of human personalities and their interactions, or when art is approached only as an aesthetic production based upon certain formal laws, then the humanities do not open to spiritual worlds but are trapped in a materialism of the spirit.

While Jung focused more on the inner world of the psyche, he made some attempts to give attention to soul operating in the outer world, an attention most clearly evidenced in his work on synchronicity. But the realm of soul in the outer world is Jung's weaker side — his work here needs supplementing. That is to say, he often begins with cultural products and traces them back to the individual soul as the reservoir of images. The needed supplement begins with the individual soul and traces its movement into the world, as a movement toward culture. Let us call this motion education. As it takes place through individuals let us call this motion learning.

* * *

In order to avoid the bias that learning involves intellectual cognition, memory, and practice of skills, I want to emphasize the role of the body in learning. The impulse for learning originates in an alluring display of the beauty of the world, which evokes desire for intimate connection with the soul of the world. Things draw us to intimate knowledge as if they need us for their completion. The beauty of the world draws the soul out of an inclination toward self-enclosing mastery of the world through disengagement and into engagement with reality. This living desire to experience the world pulsing through the body wants to initiate in us a care for all things. When things are approached with the care of soul, their soul shines forth. In the ancient world each thing was seen as inhabited by a daemon, a kind of intermediary between the gods and the earthly world. Proclus said: "What we see is not the 'god' himself, but an emanation from him which is partly mortal, partly divine, and even this we do not see with our physical eyes but with the eyes of our astral body, according to the principle 'like is perceived by like'." Learning is the discipline required to awaken the astral or soul body, the capacity to perceive the outer world as image. The central task of learning is not accumulation of information, but learning to learn. This process consists of coming to realize the individual body in conjunction with the body of the world and to appreciate the conjunction as container and reflector of soul. The mythological utterances telling the stories of the world soul are the disciplines — all the arts and sciences, philosophy, poetry, history, and mathematics. That these disciplines today do not seem to carry mythical import does not mean that the daemons are absent; it does indicate that the body is bypassed in learning so that only the outer skeleton and not the image forms the material for education today.

The daemons, who are imaginal guardians of the soul of things, are also guardians of the astral body; individuals are also accompanied through life by such beings, known as geniuses. The relation between individual genius and those daemons of the world, the push and pull between them, seems to me to lie at the heart of learning. The personal genius is attracted to its similars among the daemons in the world, and thus the act of knowing through soul, the desire to be united with the things known, is the strongest factor in learning. Today we equate genius with extraordinary ability, as if it were the possession of a gifted few; this is a mistake perpetuated in schools through programs for the gifted and talented. But we each have our genius. For example, one's astrological chart gives images of the particular sectors of the world with which one's genius is congenial or not so congenial. (The Greek word mathesis, learning, can specifically also mean astrology.) A yielding to one's genius allows the impulse of learning to be released.

Those who more fully allow themselves to be inhabited by their daemon, who no longer seek to control and keep it repressed but take on the vocation of developing it are true teachers. They are teachers because they cannot stop learning; they experience a kind of possession, a madness. In a recent film, *Teachers*, a call is put in for a substitute teacher for a high school history class. Unknown to the recruiter, the man who answers the phone is not the substitute teacher but an inmate in a mental institution who happily responds to the opportunity for early release. He becomes united with the soul of the history classroom by costuming himself as historical figures — as Lincoln, Washington, General Custer — thereby engaging the students in the lessons. This teacher was not utilizing a ploy, a trick, a kind of audiovisual aid to illustrate history. He became those figures. When he is finally discovered to be a lunatic, the men with the white coats are called in and he is hauled away. As the attendants drag him down the corridor, the man exhorts them to take their hands off him and treat him with respect, for, he says, "I am a teacher." Now, in the whole high school, it seems to me, this man was in fact the only teacher. The hero of the film is supposed to be the real teacher, but he is more of a social worker, getting himself involved in all the personal problems of the students. Others are involved in school politics, or concerned with keeping discipline, or engaged in lobbying for the union or satisfying the superintendent. Only this one madman is hospitable to the spirits. The madman is the genius —sometimes.

* * *

Having located learning on the side of the body, I have to go on now and propose that one of the greatest blocks to learning is what has come to be called the mind. The mind, or thought, when not in healthy connection with the soul body rests comfortably in the illusion of knowing. The mind caught by this illusion is unwilling to learn, unwilling to be penetrated by what it does not already think that it understands. It resists even temporary confusion. This mind is like a censor or a watchdog, keeping learning from happening. It lets through only those aspects of the new that are familiar. Often mind does this brilliantly, and the one who is least able to learn appears the most capable and does the best within the system. Let us in fact call this the superiority complex of learning, a pathology of learning that keeps soul away through cleverness. Burnout results from education that is oriented only toward the mind. It is a symptom that indicates that learning has been misplaced, that it has no body, and that the mythical creatures of learning, the geniuses, have been tamed by the ego of learning.

* * *

Every true teacher knows there is a secret erotic life to teaching; and every true learner is in love with the teacher. Yet the subject of the connection between teacher and learner is taboo, and everything possible intervenes to break this relationship — computers, programmed instruction, television, audiovisual aids, self-paced learning, films, slides. But if learning through soul is on the side of the body, the relationship between teacher and learner constitutes an unavoidable subject. Technical learning — either when the instrumentation actually teaches or when the teacher becomes no more than a technical device, an organizer and transmitter of information — cannot be seen as an advance in education. Such a reduction to technique suppresses the soul of learning. Technical education attempts to teach without body. It assumes the learner to be without body, to be anybody and nobody. To learn through soul, one must see through the eyes of the heart, love the subject matter as one sees the teacher loving it. This learning first comes to consciousness as a love for the teacher and makes possible a love of that which one studies, awakening the world as image. True learning makes one vulnerable to the intoxication of love; when one is in love one is learning, the two conditions cannot be separated. The love between teacher and learner is directed not toward possessing each other, but toward caring for the world. It is precisely here that teaching becomes an art, the art of enlarging love to encompass the soul of the world.

Through the mediation of the love between teacher and learner, genius becomes united with skill. That is to say, when one feels love, the skills necessary to adequately articulate that love will follow, will be worked on to be developed. The particular attractions to the world forming one's genius need the development of skill. Skills cannot be taught separate from the sense of genius, and genius cannot be engendered without love. In the Middle Ages myth was often used as allegory to explain certain notions; this was a misuse of myth but nevertheless helpful in describing realities of the soul. The myth of Orpheus and Euridice was employed to describe the relation between skill and learning. Orpheus, the most famous poet and musician who ever lived, was struck by Eros and fell in love with Euridice. On their wedding day, Euridice was bitten on the ankle by a poisonous snake and descended immediately into the underworld, there to be met by old, wise Aristeus. Orpheus grieved at the loss and descended into Hades to recover Euridice. With his music Orpheus charmed Hades and Persephone and even moved the furies to weeping. Euridice was returned to Orpheus on the condition that as she followed him out of Hades he could not look back upon her until they reached the upperworld. As they approached daylight, Orpheus looked back to see if Euridice was still there, and so lost her forever. Orpheus then wandered the world, playing music on the lyre.

The allegorical interpretation of the myth identified Euridice as genius, Orpheus as skill, the snake as concupiscence, and Aristeus as a wise old man, a philosopher. When genius falls into "mere body," into desire, it dies. Skill cannot live without genius and genius cannot live without skill. Without Euridice, Orpheus is the mere voice of music without its genius. Without Orpheus, Eurydice is connected to profound thought without body. Orpheus' mistake in looking back into the underworld to see if Eurydice is following him is the mistake of putting skill ahead of genius. The story indicates that love, which holds together skill with genius must remain the most important, but also the most unselfconscious element of learning. Bringing love into the discussion of learning risks revealing something that needs to remain mysterious. For this reason nothing more will be said concerning its operation.

* * *

I want to examine two basic skills, reading and writing, bringing genius back into relation with skill through love. It is a matter of looking upon skill from the place of

Euridice. The myth does not say Euridice cannot look upon Orpheus, only that Orpheus cannot look back at Euridice.

A book is an extraordinary object, unlike any other utilitarian object, because it is able to cast a spell over us. It performs magic. Through the book we are transported into some other place. We may be sitting in a chair or at a desk, but when we open a book and begin reading we are in another world; the astral or soul body perceives that other world. It may seem that television constitutes a similar form of magic, and that the book is on its way to obsolescence. Television transports us into another world and requires no effort. However, television disembodies the viewer in a way that the book does not disembody the reader. Everything is provided with television: sound, image, character, plot. Television requires no inner work, and because no work is done, no transformation of the viewer can occur.

Reading is a form of work, of soul work. As such it involves body, mind, soul, spirit — not just the disembodied perceptual apparatus mirroring what presents itself. Every time we read, a secondary making occurs; reading constitutes a part of the creation of the book itself. A book needs a reader in order to be a book. Without a reader, the book is a lifeless object.

When we read we say words. In saying the words we perform a magical act, an incantation that brings forth the appearance of a world. A book does not consist of a series of words, sentences, paragraphs, pages, chapters from the viewpoint of the genius of reading. The genius of reading looks upon the structure of the book as the necessary medium, the messengers casting the spell, transporting us into a world of image.

To read it is necessary to give in to the incantations, to take them in fully in an act of naive trust not unlike the yielding to the advances of a lover. The book cannot do its work in the face of reserve, when approached for what we can get out of it; the magic works through our getting into it. A book is a way of reading the world by letting the world play over us.

Reading is an action of the body, an art of the eyes. In reading, the eyes must be educated into touching, smelling, tasting, thinking, moving, hearing, speaking, and feeling, at the level of soul. And because reading engages the soul of the world, reading affects the world. The world would not be the same if there were no readers; without the support of readers, the world would fall into an impulsive mass, a chaotic confusion set up for takeover by mass media. Reading constitutes a care for the world, touching it ever so lightly, caressing it with the eyes, dancing with it, smelling and hearing its invisible shapes.

Reading also terrifies. As the body moves out of its biological innocence and into the mysteries of a soul engagement with the world, we feel violated, transgressed. The intellectualization of reading renders safe again that which is not meant to be safe. It reduces the world to a textbook of neutral knowledge. Textbook writers, like censors, protect the reader from the complexities of soul. Textbooks are to be avoided, for they have the purpose of anesthetizing soul.

Reading, in the sense explored here, cannot be taught as a matter of technical skill. It must come from one who has learned to read, one who knows the mysteries of reading. It must come from an artisan of reading, a lover not of books, but of the world. One who knows how to employ the magical instrument of books to open new perception of the world — that one enlivens the world soul. The world has found its way into the book as a place through which it appears as image. Much of education concerns itself with the prevention of true reading by touting reading as a basic skill. Reading is on the way to becoming a secret art.

We listen with our eyes when reading and speak with our hands when writing. The mystery of writing concerns the manner in which soul finds its way through the mechanics of grammar to rise up from the page speaking that which no single word can, what the series of words does not say, but what can only be said through them. Where do words come from, those that reluctantly ooze from the pen? Even if we may say that we have learned them, where do they come from at the moment of need? They are not stored in the brain as in a file cabinet, not even as on a computer disk. Words reside with us everywhere, available as if in the air for speaking. The world is the word that passes through us and out again in the act of speaking and writing. Through the process an intermingling of individual soul and world soul results. If this intermingling did not occur the world would surely die, following the laws of entropy.

The first lesson in writing through soul is getting around the editor accompanying us in our attempts to set down what cannot be said. Actually, there are many editors, imaginal beings whose task consists of seeing to it that world does not get transformed into word; the moral editor, the family editor, the society editor, the public relations editor — all saying, no that is not the right way. The anxiety produced by the editors alters when the hope of saying something to the world changes into the desire for the world to say what it needs to say through the word. A writer may feel he has a message he wishes to communicate, but really the words are using him to get what they want. The point of writing, of its struggles, pains, hurts, is to lose oneself in the word, to remove oneself from what one writes so that it can live.

* * *

There is much talk these days about vocational learning, but little concerning learning as vocation. The purpose of learning through soul is not to prepare for a vocation, a job, or a profession, because learning itself is a vocation. It does not belong to the young, does not concern itself with utility or even with self-enrichment. Learning is for the sake of the soul of the world, unending steps taken to support the inherent animation of all things, visible and invisible. The purpose of learning is not to get something but to give something, to release learning into the world, there to mingle and make entanglement, complexity that at the same time enlivens. Life and the world are simpler without learning. We long for that simplicity, wish that we had not learned and that the world were not so complex. What is this fear of complexity? If we could get closer to that fear, face it, it would no longer produce the twofold desire for simplicity on the one hand and a technologizing of the world as an attempt to control complexity on the other. That is to say, romanticizing the simple world and seeking control through technological means amount to the same thing, a response of fear to the ensouled world. Learning is a form of action, dramatic in form, the world finding its way into plot, story, tension, soul. Learning has the power of changing the world, but in unknown ways, producing unpredictable outcomes. All learning tells a story of the world and produces images of what the world is like in its action. True learning sets one free because it sets the world free, acknowledges the world's own voice, allows it to speak, making incessant change.

* * *

The endeavor to bring about learning through soul belongs primarily to adult education. Presently there are no forms for this kind of learning because care for the soul has become incarcerated in the institution of psychotherapy. What should occur in life psychotherapy places in the interaction between two or more individuals in an artificial situation. Why artificial? There is nothing whatsoever within the soul that would call forth a particular cultivation of soul called psychotherapy. Friendship and the intimacy of a love relationship may come to mind, but neither of these forms takes place in an isolated chamber, and even friends and lovers do not know what a therapist knows because a therapist knows what he should not.

Psychotherapy is an abstraction, sanctioned, more or less, by society in a world of materialistic abstractions. Learning, however, as it has been described here, belongs to the very nature of living, and only when removed from the world produces the self — perpetuating illness of psychotherapy. Once a theory of the unconscious is established, a psychic iatrogenesis ensues. That is, the cure of illness becomes the source of illness. The theory perpetuates itself, and what begins as a limited field spreads into a cultural phenomenon. Psychotherapy is a self-perpetuating phenomenon; the more it is done, the more illness is created. The missing element in present culture is an education into the life of soul. Adult education would restore to culture knowledge of the soul. Presently, adult education is oriented either toward furtherance of technical skills or toward personal enrichment. Where then is to be found an education of the soul today? There isn't one because the imitation, the double, of such a task occurs as psychotherapy. That is to say, real soul knowledge has no culture. Cultural forms are needed for the cure. Psychotherapy cannot do the job and seems to me to be a deviation contributing to the destruction of culture.

The method of soul learning is quite different than education of the young, for the task of cultural learning is much more placed in the hands of the learners and with a community of learners. The teacher is not as important and must be skilled enough to recede into the background while nonetheless serving as a guide who can help shape the vessel and restrain the learning from wandering into personal subjectivity. Adult education is a community learning but is in no sense a group psychotherapy. The method of such learning is meditative rather than intellectual, for soul learning is an education into subtlety. Adult education must also be distinguished from reading or study groups. Such groups tend to be oriented toward detailed understanding of a particular work or text and foster a strengthening of the intellect rather than the soul. What the teacher of soul learning must first gain and then sacrifice is the development of intellect. As such soul teaching occurs in practice, the teacher actually has much knowledge and information, but it is knowledge and information the teacher cannot give forth. The teacher does not withhold it, but brings it into the learning situation to be given up, in order to provide the milieu for the meditative learning pursued by the community of learners. Reading is approached in a similarly meditative manner. The teacher encourages reading that takes place through picture consciousness rather than through the grasping of concepts. Such reading and study is not directed toward what the learner can take away from the text but toward the immersing of self in text in a living way. The learner must give life to the images in the text. Needless to say, this form of learning is noncompetitive. No evaluation takes place, no examinations or grades are given. Such devices would stimulate the wrong forces for soul learning.

Is there a curriculum for the soul? A crucial question. Yes, there is material, but it is not a sequentially arranged form of study that progresses from the simple to the more complex. Secondary texts are avoided, and as well the use of excerpts from works, because the aim is to become immersed not in what is said about some topic, but in the reality itself. Art forms are of particular importance for an education into soul. Myth, fairy tale, story, symbolic imagery, poetry, drama, painting, music, and film — are approached not as expression of an inner psyche but as events of the world soul. Then the learner can move to things of the everyday world — architecture, medicine, science, even mathematics — when it is possible to approach such things through image.

* * *

Of what practical use is learning through soul? I suspect that there are four kinds of learning: 1. There is learning for the sake of use. This way of learning develops the technical sensibility. 2. There is learning for the sake of learning.

This mode develops the scholarly sensibility. 3. There is learning that seeks for the good life. This learning develops the humanistic imagination, a concern for humanity as a whole. 4. Then there is the learning of soul, learning as love, not love of learning. This way of learning develops the imagination, it unites the inner forum of individual soul with the objects of the outer world. As such it is as "useless" as art. Why seek to develop such a form of learning? The alternatives are: to seek a use for learning and to develop technology; to seek to use imagination, to become a magician exercising imaginative power, thereby depriving others of their freedom; to use learning for power; to give up the question of use and take learning to be a new form of mysticism. I find none of these alternatives satisfying. I can best describe what I mean — when I say that learning through soul is as useless as art — by saying that the aim of soul learning is to increase porosity.

Porosity (coming from the word porous) is the ratio between what one takes in and what one gives out. The aim of learning through soul is to increase porosity on the side of giving out and to reduce it on the side of taking in. This is not an abstract process but something that can be seen in the world. Our sun is the best instance of porosity that gives out and does not take in. Our sun is a star, and all of the stars give out without taking in. In this act we find our homeland. We might imagine this kind of learning as the making of the treasured philosopher's stone of the alchemists. What is the philosopher's stone? One alchemical text, the *Gloria Mundi* says . . . "the stone is familiar to all men, both young and old; it is found in the country, in the village and in the town, in all things created; yet it is despised by all. Rich and poor handle it every day. It is cast into the street by servant maids. Children play with it. Yet no one prized it, though it is the most beautiful and precious thing upon the earth and has power to pull down kings and princesses. Nevertheless, it is esteemed the vilest and meanest of terrestrial things." I dare say, this stone is the soul of the world. How impotent and insignificant it seems. The purpose of learning through soul concerns the intensification of what is actually present, which comes about when individual soul conjoins with world soul. This conjunction occurs as word. Whenever the expressions of the world meet with the expressions of the individual the resonant quality of the world intensifies. Here we touch upon another quality of the soul of the world, that of sound.

Soul learning does not consist of the internalization of knowledge, the determination of right meaning, the achievement of accuracy, but is to be found in what sounds right. That soul sings was understood by the ancient psychology of the soul of the world — the singing of soul was known as the music of the spheres. At one time it was possible for the cosmos to play as music and for the imagination to hear it. The movement of the planets in their relation to each other could be heard. According to John Lash the reality of the sounding universe formed the basis for meditation practices. In the Vedic traditions, the source of the Veda is *Vak*, the creative word. Vak is a feminine noun derived from the verb *Vach*, to enunciate or speak. In both the Vedas and the Tantras, *Vak* is considered as both the source of creation and the all-pervading basis of manifest phenomena. It is the primal and originating word power, dwelling in all things.

In the Brihadaranyaka Upanishad, *Vak* is identified with Shabda-Brahman. *Shabda* means sound-current or sound-torrent. *Brahman* is the name for the supreme creative principle, coming from the root *brih*, to expand. So, *Shabda-Brahman* is the sound-torrent of the creative-expansive principle. The Vedic-Tantric teachings point back to the remote era when the soul of the world filled all space. To put it more precisely, sound was space. To be filled with pure sound was to be held in the world soul. This cosmic hum is epitomized in the mantra-syllable OM. In later gnostic Christian writing, *Vak* is found as Logos, the Word. Among the gnostics, the Logos is considered as feminine and identified with Sophia. In the New Testament, the gospel of St. John, a thoroughly gnostic text, opens with the declaration: "In the beginning was the

Word, and the Word was the God, and the Word was with God." The important and neglected statement of this declaration — "and the Word was with God" — refers to Sophia. Now, however, the voice of the world soul remains silent, drowned out by the monotheism of the Father Logos.

The voice of soul remained occluded until rediscovered by Jung in his experimental studies on word association in 1909. The word association studies employ a series of stimulus words to which subjects are asked to respond. The reactions do not come with equal smoothness, but vary irregularly in terms of length of response intervals. Jung found that the response to stimulus words was often based on sound rather than meaning. A response based on meaning, for example, would be "flower" to the stimulus "bloom." Examples of responses to "bloom" based on sound would be "bloomer" or "blood." The great disparity between the magnificent sense of the cosmos as sound in the Vedic teachings and this small and seemingly insignificant resounding of soul in words makes one inclined to want to visit the local Zen center rather than the world — an instance of the attracting power of illusion. The cosmos has fallen into silence; if it is to sound again, it must come from the small sounds of soul. To practice ancient methods of connecting with soul does not, I believe, produce an experience of soul, but rather a remembrance of what soul experiences were once like. Such remembrances are powerful, even though the powers they recall are no longer effective in the cosmos, but they take one away from the work of seeking soul within the present world. The very small voice of soul rediscovered by Jung indicates the necessity now of developing soul through learning daily to speak the things of the world, through gradually amplifying those resonances. The intensity of the experience of learning through soul does not count as much as the regularity of practice. Soul learning is a mode of living toward world soul that is to be carried out in daily life.

LETTER IV

Disease

DEAR FRIEND,

I want to speak of disease, letting disease tell the condition of soul in the world. In order for disease to speak in this way, the modern medical attitude must be suspended. There are many aspects to this modern outlook: the viewing of the body as a conglomeration of parts, of disease as the invasion of the body by destructive entities, of the physician as heroic warrior; the assumption that death is evil; the optimism that the marriage between science and technology will produce cures of all diseases, disease itself being seen as evil. This outlook now extends far beyond the bounds of medicine and constitutes a way of looking upon everything in the world that we find uncomfortable or do not like. Everything from drinking to sex to relationships that are difficult now counts as disease and thus as being in need of medical treatment. I want to approach disease from an entirely different standpoint, to give it a hearing as a presentation of the soul of the world, and I shall concentrate on three epidemics of the present world — AIDS, cancer, and heart attack.

These three maladies are quite unlike the diseases of the past. From ancient times until the nineteenth century most disease involved the quality of heat, illness characterized by fever to be gone through. We vaguely remember such illnesses — whooping cough, pneumonia, measles, small pox, diphtheria. There was actually little the physician could do other than guide the patient through the fever, which was understood as a cleansing and also an awakening of soul because fever is often accompanied by visions, strange dreams, hallucination. Fever is a heat that stimulates image. The onset of inoculations and antibiotics changed the understanding of fever. With these weapons twentieth century medical doctors have learned to fight against disease rather than working with the body's own healing abilities. Homeopathy and naturopathic medicine view the conquering of diseases of inflammation not as an advance but as an illusion. They hold that such ways of treating illness have merely driven disease deeper. It no longer appears possible to find an individual relation to the experience of falling ill because the inner forces of soul are no longer understood as engaged in a relation with disease; instead disease is treated from the outside, technically. The result is this: since the nineteenth century the form of disease has dramatically shifted away from warmth to cold. Fever is not a central part of AIDS, cancer, or heart-attack, which are better characterized as hard, cold, materialistic, opportunistic, more mechanical. It is quite feasible that this shift was brought about by medicine itself, for the progress of medicine has been in exactly the same direction. Unless modern medicine is brought into question it is not possible to give disease a hearing, so I want to further this questioning, just to the point where it is possible to free disease from the medical bias. The aim of this doubt concerning modern medicine is also to make clear how we all suffer from the infection of modern medicine.

Our modern view of disease is indebted to Louis Pasteur, who, while he did not originate the germ theory, seemed to advance it to practical application. The germ theory, now extended to viruses, holds that disease is an invasion of the body from the outside by bacteria, each disease being characterized by a distinct malignant biological entity. So established is this view that we can hardly think otherwise about the origin of illness. This theory has been suitable for our circumstances for the past one hundred years. It matches the materialism of the age. As materialists it is easy for us to understand the superficial notion of a bacterium as a foreign material entering the body and bringing about disruption of a physical, chemical proccss.

Working at the same time as Pasteur was another equally important medical researcher, Pierre Jacques Antoine Bechamp. Bechamp, working entirely independently of Pasteur, found incontrovertible evidence that germs do not infect the body from the outside as causal agents. He found that at most, they are secondary agents. Bechamp saw that germs do not come from the outside into an innocent body, which then has to be fortified by artificially stimulating it to mobilize an army to attack the invaders. He showed in fact that the body is filled with bacteria, and that bacteria have the capacity to transform themselves into an endless variety of forms. A round bacteria, for example, can turn into an oblong bacteria, and that one in turn can transform itself into something even smaller. He could not see these smaller activities, which are now called viruses. What appear as diseases are the transformations of the internal bacterial world, the submicrocosmic world. What is important in his discovery is that he was interested not in bacteria as entities but in bactcria as constant activities. He saw them not as things but functions, he saw that one must not look at separate things but at whole worlds. His view quite directly implies that the body likewise is not a thing but a complex functioning, not of multiple parts operating like a machine, but as a complete world, the soul of the world in microcosmic form. Disease then consists in an alteration by the unified bacterial world, as it reconfigures itself in relation to an alteration of the unified outer world. This elegant view accounts for particularity in relation to the whole.

To state all of this in a more practical way, for it is really a common sense point of view, we may turn to Florence Nightingale. The great pioneer of nursing saw in life what Bechamp saw under the microscope. She says:

Is it not living in a continual mistake to look upon
disease, as we do now, as separate entities, which must
exist, like cats and dogs, instead of looking upon them as
the reactions of kindly Nature against the conditions in
which we have placed ourselves? I was brought up by
scientific men to believe that smallpox was a thing of
which there was once a specimen in the world, which
went on propagating itself in a perpetual chain of de-
scent, just as much as that there was a first dog or pair of
dogs, and that smallpox would not begin itself any more
than a new dog would begin without there having been a
parent dog. Since then I have seen with my eyes and
smelt with my nose smallpox growing up in first speci-
mens, either in closed rooms or in overcrowded wards,
where it could not by any possibility have been "caught,"
but must have begun. Nay, more, I have seen diseases
begin, grow and pass into one another. Now dogs do not
pass into cats. I have seen for instance, with a little
overcrowding, continued fever grow up, and with a little
more, typhoid fever, and with a little more, typhus, and
all in the same ward or hut. For diseases, as all experience shows, are adjectives, not noun substances. The
specific disease doctrine is the grand refuge of weak,
uncultured, unstable minds, such as now rule in the
medical profession. There are no specific diseases; there
are specific disease conditions.

These two individualities, Bechamp and Nightingale,
are well worth a great deal of meditation. Do not evaluate
what they present, let the soul entertain it; it will lead to
the release of the naive medical attitude that now dominates. The profound understanding of disease offered by
these two relatively forgotten people, who had the capacity
to remain in contact with the world rather than perceive
through theory, opens the door for us to consider the trinity
of epidemic illnesses of our time, to perceive them as world
conditions, as sufferings of the soul of the world.

* * *

AIDS. Let us begin with a clinical picture of the disease of AIDS, as described by Arie Bos, an image of the phenomenon as it can be seen in everyday life, rather than the picture of AIDS as given in the more technical worlds of medicine, biology, and biochemistry. We can then try to understand what the appearance of this disease indicates concerning the situation of soul in the world.

Picture a completely emaciated man. He is completely confined to his bed, and he continuously scratches himself. Sunken cheeks, hollow temples, deep eye sockets, and fearful eyes; pale skin with festering sores; hair thin and dull, mouth and tongue covered with a white coating. He does not talk much, has no urge to make conversation, is sluggish, inhibited, and dull. This emaciated person has undergone a disintegration of bodily form. Most strikingly, the individuality of the body, what enables us to recognize a person as just that person and no other, is dulled, has almost become imperceptible. This loss of bodily integrity is due not only to the radical change of physical presence, but is combined with the dulling of the interior life, so that the individual soul seems weak.

Preceding the outbreak of AIDS, the image of AIDS related complex — ARC — consists of fever, night sweats, diarrhoea, and diminution of intellect. Immediate memory is dulled. There may be memories from early childhood, but often what happened just a few moments ago cannot be recalled. The dulling of memory is the loss of the unique set of images and concepts that makes up a person's individuality. Consciousness and the emotions also become shallow. Gestures and facial expressions, from which the emotions can be read, become shallow, as if they were disappearing. Then, on the other side, the night sweats, diarrhoea, indicate that the body can no longer hold its form; it is as if the body were dissolving.

This picture reveals AIDS as the gradual disintegration of both body and soul, of the soul body. The creating activities that bring about the physical manifestation of soul out of the invisible soul world — these activities cease.

This disintegration applies to the four soul elements composing the earthly world, including the body — Earth, Water, Air, Fire. The structural individuality of the physical body, or Earth, no longer holds. The Water element of the body, in which the physiological processes of cells take place, fall apart. The inbreathing and outbreathing of the lungs, and the flow of the blood, that through the Air element form a continual relationship between inside and outside become subject to opportunistic infection. The processes that maintain the inner warmth or Fire of the body grow weak. These four elemental worlds, not the substances we now know by these names, have since ancient times been recognized as the creating soul elements of the earth. With AIDS these elemental worlds go their own way, so to speak, and without their coherence each of the creative elements of the soul body is subject to every possible malign influence. With AIDS it is not that soul withdraws, as in the case of all death; but the body-making activity of soul disappears as if it had evaporated, just as in the situation of the present world the importance of soul has evaporated. One might argue that what I have called soul is no more than a vague, mystical term for the processes of the immune system, which science is on the way to understanding with ever greater precision. However, then we no longer hear the disease, but are already caught by the desire to get rid of it. The immune system functions to maintain the boundary between what belongs to bodily integrity and what is alien to this integrity and belongs to the outside world. Thus, the medical argument says AIDS is a disfunction of the immune system. Holding to this argument, and by it coming to the invention of drugs such as AZT, which, incidentally, destroys the life force, takes us off on a wrong track. It is the wrong track because the logic is wrong. If one cannot see what is actually present but instead follows materialistic theories, then one is like a person walking along a road who upon discovering footprints says that they are due to the ground rather than to the other person who left them. When we trust what is immediately present, then an unavoidable conclusion arises: AIDS is a disease of soul, it is the disappearance of soul in the world.

If we take the clinical picture of AIDS as an image of the condition of the world, we come to the following diagnosis. The present age is characterized by a physical deteriorating of the structures of culture and by a loss of soul. Anonymity abounds with a pervasive incapacity to experience individuality. There is a memory of the way things used to be, but the loss of day to day memory makes it impossible to find continuity of experience. Emotional life becomes shallow, the will absent, the interior life lost. These disappearing qualities belonged first to the world; the world's suffering and the neglect of that suffering are secondarily manifested through the microcosmic world of the individual body.

The most successful treatment of Aids-related illness that I have been able to locate is the work of Dr. Jesse Stoff. One can hardly call it medical treatment. First, Dr. Stoff concentrates on sleep pattern, altering the sufferer's pattern to align with maximum regenerative time of sleep. Then the doctor focuses on exercise, exercise that is not muscle bound but rhythmic and meditative. Then natural, not synthetic vitamins and minerals are used, along with homeopathic remedies. Finally, the care program avoids toxic foods. Over 90 percent of the people with chronic fatigue syndrome who have followed this treatment have experienced apparently permanent remission.

If we look at each aspect of the procedure, what shows forth is the fact that rhythm is brought into the lives of these patients — through sleep, movement, living, vitalizing food elements, and homeopathic remedies (which are not chemical substances at all but the essences of substances, made through rhythmic steps of successive dilution, to the point that not a molecule of the actual substance remains in the final remedy). The success of this treatment suggests that what the world lacks is rhythm and feeling, and when rhythm and feeling are absent the center cannot hold. That is to say, when the world is turned into a noun the adjectival world soul disintegrates. Rhythm, characteristic of soul, must now be given back to the world through our engagement in the world with soul.

If we begin by looking at disease as a manifestation of the soul of the world the conclusion is clear, it is common sense. Anything used to attack a disease from the outside also attacks the whole body; that is to say, any attempt to cure a disease by an outside agent is bound to produce other diseases that are alterations of the first. Disease is our fundamental condition, our built-in psychotherapist, our constant advisor, our ever faithful guru — it is always ready to tell us what we need to do in life. If we but ask, it is there to show us what is missing in the world.

* * *

CANCER. Cancer is the most substantial, most concrete, instance of the suffering of the things of the world, a suffering belonging to the body of the world before it belongs to the body of the individual. While actual cancer is pervasive, cancerphobia is now universal, producing morbid fear of everything in the world; which is to say that everything in the world is in fear. The medical overlay of these fears diverts attention away from the psychic suffering of things to the falsely heroic missionary conquest of a dreaded illness. The belief that medicine will conquer this disease brings about forgetfulness of the world conditions that express cancer while it simultaneously enlarges individual fears to neurotic proportions.

The list of cancerous things grows daily: cement, asphalt, wallboard, pipes, textiles, insulation, brake linings, phonograph records, floor coverings, garden hose, PVC pipes, furniture, upholstery, food wrappings, tires, octane booster, adhesives, paints, nylons, pesticides, ink, varnishes, chemicals in tobacco, dyes, saccharin, plastic bottles, and artificial sex hormones are all listed as carcinogens. Two peculiarities characterize substances determined as cancerous, which are primarily made from synthetic inorganic chemicals: they do not belong to nature, and they make possible the proliferation of mass-produced objects on a scale unheard of before. These synthetic substances possess a peculiar kind of immortality, because they are incapable of entering into the organic cycle of life and death, and when discarded they do not return to dust because from dust they did not come; they came from chemical factories. As such, they lack the true individuality of things and bear no mark of handwork. Without exception, the world of cancer is the world of mass objects rather than individual things. Cancer appears in the body as the uprising of masses of undifferentiated cells destroying the individual structure of the body. Cancer goes together with mass society.

In the tradition of homeopathic medicine, disease consists of the materialization in the body of imagination belonging to worldly things. Oswald Croll, Paracelsus' student, states: "Man is a hidden world, because visible things in him are invisible, and when they are made visible, then they are diseases, as truly as he is the little world and not the great one." If we look more closely at the formation of tumors, we can see what is becoming visible, constituting the disease. A tumor is more than a proliferation of cells; this aspect of the illness only shows how we are caught by the world of mass objects. Upon close examination a malignant mass shows form. A "ripe" cancer of the ovaries, for example, is not a formless growth, but often shows fully formed teeth. Other cancerous cavities exhibit the growth of hair, or of brain tissue. A body is trying to materialize in cancer. But it is a freakish body, a body without the forming capacities of soul. Cancer reveals that the world is being treated as a mere material thing, and that the project of modern life is the forming of a double, imitation world that has now extended even as far as the human body.

Any cancer that shows itself as a bodily condition is already an old cancer; in fact, the appearance of a tumor indicates the terminal phase of the disease. Approaching cancer after it already materializes in the body may be looking in the wrong place in the wrong way. Medicine gives little attention to pre-cancerous symptoms. The more subtle aspects of the disease give a clear indication of what is going on in the soul of the world. Victor Bott finds two invariable pre-indicators of cancer. The first is the onset of fatigue that will not go away, a particular kind of fatigue unlike exhaustion from work and also unlike depression. The fatigue can be described as more like a lack of animation, an inability to feel engaged in the world. The second symptom is insomnia. Bott says: "One could even say that any insomnia beginning without evident cause must make one suspect latent cancer." Only to the materialist eye do these symptoms appear as signs of the body under attack by a deadly enemy, by some unknown virus. The fatigue of the natural body, the stressed-out body, that no longer finds the world a home, calls for a different kind of engagement with the world — an engagement alert to all that is unnatural in the world, alert to the dying body of the world, committed to enlivening the world, to reclothing it with acts of imagination. The symptom of insomnia points in a similar direction. The inability to sleep, to enter into the dream world, suggests the necessity of seeing the world through the spontaneous act of image making characteristic of dreaming.

The suggestion that cancer indicates the need for the activation of an imagination of the world in no way implies a new sort of medicine. The medical attitude makes us forgetful of the world itself as suffering loss of soul. If the view I have suggested were immediately taken over into a medical view, it would result in the application of personal imagery as a way of countering one's own cancer. While such a direction would have many advantages over the invasion of the body through surgery or chemotherapy, the world would be left unattended, without the application of soul forces that could gradually regenerate its soul.

* * *

HEART ATTACK. Heart attack relates to the world in panic, the world that has lost rhythm, pace, tone, the world in anxiety. The Greek word for anxiety is *mermeros*, meaning division of an entity into smaller and smaller portions — dismemberment, that is. The Latin word for anxiety is *angor*, meaning strangling. I suspect that we have received our word "anger" from this source, as well as the word "angina," the narrowing of the arteries, the anxiety of the heart no longer connected to the flow of time. Smoking, drinking, overeating, lack of exercise — these behaviors cannot be taken as reasons for heart failure, for they serve merely as means to cover deep anxiety, anxiety that belongs first to the dismembered, angry, narrow world in which there is no connection between one thing and another. Does not anxiety come when there are too many things to pay attention to, when there are too many disconnected demands, producing limitation in the field of attention, an underlying apathy, depression of spirit, a wish to keep the world with all its demands at bay through excessive control? Anxiety, then, connects with the attempt to keep the anxious world away from the body. Ironically, a culture that keeps the world separate from the body produces the artificial heart, the heart that locates the world-as-object right at the center of the body. Thus far, such a procedure has not been able to sustain life, while borrowing the hearts of others has prolonged it.

Before the onset of the metaphor of the heart as a pump, heart was felt throughout the body as the rhythmic activity of the body. The pump changes rhythm into mechanical circulation, as activity in the world is also viewed as mechanical circulation — of money, goods, ideas, traffic, water. The idea of circulation goes together with the idea of progress; progress does not advance culture, but keeps the same old things circulating in more and more mechanical, automated ways while no substantial transformation ever takes place. With progress what begins as heart becomes more and more brain; the activity of the brain now determines life and death.

The heart is the organ of imagination. A man does not think of his lover first and then remember her. He feels her presence first, and then he may go on to think about her. To reverse this produces a kind of schizophrenia. For the brain, heart is not only a pump but a muscle, and the schizoid state consists of the attempt to control the course of love instead of yielding to it. To conceive of the heart as a muscle or a pump attributes to the brain a priority that it does not have — the realization of love, the production of the desired feeling, is linked to the control of external things, and the feeling disappears the moment control is brought into question. Most of the muscles of the body depend on a nerve connection to the brain for activation; and likewise, a pump requires some external source of power. But while the rhythm of the heart requires stimulation, it does not rely on the brain. The wave that starts and keeps the heart beating comes from a tiny bundle of tissue in the right atrium, the sinoatrial node, the pacemaker of the heart. The heart has a mind of its own; it knows what to do without orders from above, just as someone who knows what is in her heart does not require directions concerning what to do and how to act. The heart stimulates imagination and produces the actions of imagination, the creation of fantasy. Cardiac arrhythmias may not be particularly serious, but they may be a sign that the heart's rhythms are being neglected. Those rhythms do not belong to that physical organ in the chest, but to the rhythm of the world, even to the rhythm of the cosmic world. Rudolf Steiner shows the relation of the rhythm of the cosmos to the rhythm of the body in the following manner. A human being takes approximately eighteen breaths a minute, which comes to 1,080 breaths an hour, or 25,920 breaths a day. An ordinary life span is about 70 years. The number of days in 70 years is approximately 25,500. A cosmic year is 25,900 years. The cosmic year is described by Plato in the Timaeus; he calls it the perfect year, as was calculated by Protagoras. It is derived this way: the number of years it will take before the sun again rises at exactly the same moment as it does today is 25,920. These intriguing calculations point to the way in which the rhythm of the body is related to the rhythm of the cosmos. We do not recognize this correspondence because the periodicity is different. The rhythm of a lifetime corresponds to the rhythm of the cosmic year. Because of the difference in periodicity we are somewhat free from the rhythms of the cosmos; in ancient times people experienced these relationships directly for they had access to the experience of their blood and could perceive its relation to the surrounding world. The development of intellectual consciousness dimmed this experience, which is no longer directly given but must be reimagined.

The loss of the experience of the blood may be related to the anesthetizing of the arteries through cholesterol. The liver and intestines produce cholesterol all the time — just the amount the body needs. So, if an excess of cholesterol is connected with heart failure, we must look into this factor of coronary artery disease. Brendan Phibbs says that coronary artery disease is the great epidemic of the twentieth century, the "black death" of our time. Over 100 million Americans have some degree of coronary artery disease, which is described as a symptomless disorder characterized by the thickening and deteriorizing of the blood supply conduits to the heart. Cholesterol in the body is primarily responsible for insulating the electrical activities of the brain, one from the other, so that we do not short-circuit ourselves. Cholesterol is also a necessary component for the rigidity of cell walls. That cholesterol should be a factor in heart attack tells us something about the present world — a world that is excessively isolating and rigid, a world in which the processes of the brain have entered into the whole body, requiring additional insulation there. Arterial blockage, over time, makes the heart beat not only harder but louder. The heart continually makes a sonic image; the heart is the only organ that can be continually heard. Daniel Schneider reports, for example, a case of a man who kept having recurring dreams of a woman sitting at a sewing machine, incessantly sewing. The dreamer always awoke filled with fear of having a heart attack. Schneider takes the visual image to be a transformation of a sonic image of the heart, and he even locates the image as the dreamer hearing his own heart resounding from the pillow on which he lay sleeping. When rhythm is replaced by mechanism in the world, the heart resounds fear.

We can begin reimagining our relation to the larger cosmos by recognizing the anxious state of the world. The poet Frank O'Hara gives an indication of the anxious state of the world, and the needed response: "My eyes are a vague blue, like the sky, and change all the time: they are indiscriminate but fleeting, entirely specific and disloyal, so that no one trusts me. I am always looking away. Or again at something after it has given me up. It makes me restless and that makes me unhappy, but I cannot keep them still. . . . It's not that I'm curious. On the contrary, I am bored, but it is my duty to be attentive. I am needed by things as the sky must be above the earth. And lately so great has their anxiety become, I can spare myself little sleep."

To place ourselves within the rhythms of the cosmos we must face the anxiety of things and feel their panic, doing so with fully conscious imagining — not going to dreams or art or analysis, but to the world, there not to avoid anxiety but to go through it. We need to ask what this deep anxiety wants from us — where and how does it want to go — not how to sidestep it.

Let us review the situation of the heart to see if it is possible to hear what the anxiety of heart attack suggests as a way back into the soul of the world. When brain is imposed upon heart, anxiety is provoked; the pace of the brain has replaced the rhythm of the heart; the personal heart, the romantic heart, perpetuates the heart-brain split; the circulation model of the world is fast breaking down.

Return to the statement that the heart is the organ of imagination; this is more than a figure of speech. When we say imagination belongs to the heart, but do not mean the physical organ of the heart, it is an expression of sentimentalism. Imagination in the sentimental sense does not go as deep as our physiology; it is no more than a shadowy idea with emotional overtones. It is possible, however, to enter into an experience of the heart, directly, beginning with feeling its rhythm, feeling its contraction and expansion. Then, it is possible to go inside with careful concentration. One finds an inner space, not an empty space, but quite clearly a quiet chamber. And each time the heart pulses, there is a moment of uncertainty, a little death, and from that point of absolute contraction there occurs a moment of radiation, an outpouring that even extends beyond the boundaries of the physical body. If you pay attention, you can feel this rhythm. When one attunes oneself to this rhythm the perception of the outer world changes, or more accurately, the face of the world changes into a silent world with depth. The interior of the outer world becomes perceptible. The soul of the world gradually reveals itself. The key to regeneration lies in the moment of uncertainty that takes place eighteen times a minute, for the ever-present gap that distinguishes the rhythm of the heart from the continuous roll of the machine locates vulnerability as essential to the outpouring of the heart and to continuing creative activity within the soul of the world. We make a very large error assuming the world to be finished. The world is an ongoing creative action of soul, taking place rhythmically, in time with the rhythmic activity of heart that creates our bodies.

* * *

When disease confronts us, the most typical response is to search for a way out, whether through the treatment of standard medicine or some other more noninvasive alternative treatment. Such alternatives form a secret alliance with standard practice in conceiving of illness as wrong. The new language says something is out of balance — chakras, energy systems, emotions, or subtle bodies. This new language and practice, however, conceives of health as light and disease as darkness. No one wants to think about disease, least of all those who fear bearing it. "The fear of disease," said Paracelsus, "is more dangerous than disease itself." Do not the physicians prey on this fear, making it impossible to listen to disease? Listen again to Paracelsus:

> You physicians have entirely deserted the path indicated by nature, and built up an artificial system, which is fit for nothing but to swindle the public and to prey upon the pockets of the sick. Your safety is due to the fact that your gibberish is unintelligible to the public, who fancy that it must have a meaning, and the consequence is that no one comes near you without being cheated. Your art does not consist in curing the sick, but in worming yourself into the favor of the rich, in swindling the poor, and in gaining admittance to the kitchens of the noblemen of the country. You live upon imposture, and the aid and abetment of the legal profession enables you to carry on your impostures, and to evade punishment by the law. You poison the people and ruin their health; you are sworn to use diligence in your art; but how could you do so, as you possess no art, and all your boasted science is nothing but an invention to cheat and deceive? You denounce me because I do not follow your schools; but your schools can teach me nothing which would be worth knowing. You belong to the tribe of snakes, and I expect nothing but poison from you. You do not spare the sick; how could I expect that you would respect me, while I am cutting down your income by exposing your pretensions and ignorance to the public?

In truth, all hope in the physicians — and too, all hope in the alternative healers — must be relinquished before it is possible to hear disease as the voice of the soul of the world. When hope of conquering disease has been given up, it will be possible to return to those same practitioners with a different understanding than that of having one's body worked on or of working on one's own body. Disease may become the occasion for learning how medical treatment can become a way of caring for the soul of the world. One who goes to the doctor's office, undergoes treatment, and returns to the world facing it cxactly as before has missed an opportunity to face the world with soul.

LETTER V

Economics and Money

DEAR FRIEND,

Economics and money work together as the primary veil covering direct perception of the soul of the world. Thus, we shall have to work very hard, first to apprehend the veil itself and then to see through the veil, to see how in fact the very same thing that obscures the world soul can also provide access to it. Let us begin by tracing the manner in which economics replaces soul as the governing force of the world; then I shall attempt to recover soul in economics itself and point to ways of imagining the actions of money as integral to the recovery of the soul of the world. This path will adhere to the system of economics and money known as capitalism, but will be a revisioning of that system placing soul at the center.

Methical, systematic, continuous pursuit of gain with the avoidance of all pleasure characterizes the original spirit of capitalism. Capitalism was born of the Protestant Reformation. The great fear felt by all forms of puritanism is that somewhere, somehow, someone is having a good time. As far as I know, the relation between capitalism and modern psychology has never been explored, an apparent oversight since the two begin at the very same moment. The great Philipp Melanchthon, friend of Martin Luther, fellow theologian, supported and gave clear formulation to the respectability of restrained accumulation of capital. He also introduced the word *psychology* into the modern vocabulary. I aim to show that because of Melanchthon modern economics consists of nothing more than subjective psychology projected onto the world, an impenetrable veil that now counts as reality; that is to say, as I will show, there is nothing in the world that does not seem to be an economic matter.

Psychological sensibility has been around in the Western world since Heraclitus, *circa* 500 B.C. Psyche, or soul, permeated everything and was not limited to human beings. The world was ensouled, and economics simply meant the care of the household of the world. Heraclitus put it this way: "You could not discover the limits of the psyche, even if you traveled every road to do so, such is the depth of its meaning." The care of the household was not simple, nor automatically given as though it were some primordial contact with the beauty of nature. It took place through ritual oriented toward conforming human life to the life within the cosmos; it took place through sacrificial rites, through disciplines such as astrology coordinating the motions of the heavens with character and action; it took place through including care of all objects of the household, the city, and the environment as under the guidance of divine beings or daemonic spirits.

Melanchthon, by naming a field psychology, by limiting psyche to what goes on in individuals, stopped soul from appearing in any place but individual subjectivity; and at the same time economics changed from care of the household of the world to the pursuit of personal gain. Capitalism has come a long way — from the pursuit of limited gain with the avoidance of pleasure to the pursuit of unlimited gain in order to produce pleasure. This route of economics has changed the very order of time. No longer do we have spontaneous breakthroughs of ecstatic participation in the sacred events of the world soul. Now we have deliberate and planned manipulations of momentary pleasure, designed to quickly wear thin. Melanchthon's psychology lies behind it all. The first part of his *Loci Communes Theological* presents a simplistic model of individual psychology. He says:

> We divide man into only two parts. For there is in him a cognitive faculty, and there is also a faculty by which he either follows or flees the things he has come to know. The cognitive faculty is that by which we discern through the senses, understand, think, compare, and deduce. The faculty from which the affections arise is that by which we either turn away from or pursue the things known, and this faculty is sometimes called "will," sometimes "affection," and sometimes "appetite."

This definition of what constitutes the human soul, as if it has nothing to do with the outer world, founds the capitalistic spirit. Knowledge of what is to be done comes from cognition, not from the heart. Will, which contains the appetites, cannot be trusted and is therefore turned over to the guidance of God, guidance received not through actual contact but only through religious dogma. People may know what to do to acquire gain. That greed may enter cannot be controlled, but they may proceed as long as they have presumably turned their will over to God, pursuing gain without seeking their own pleasure.

Adam Smith's classical economics, which followed later, wrote the divine out of individual psychology and thus out of economics altogether, replacing the sacred element with propositions concerning human nature, claiming acquisition as an innate human trait. He said: "The desire of bettering our condition comes with us from the womb and never leaves us until we go to the grave." This revision of Melanchthon's psychology serves as base for his primary economic proposition: "Every individual is continuously exerting himself to find out the most advantageous employment for whatever capital he can command." Unlimited acquisition becomes respectable by interpreting it as rooted in human nature. Such an interpretation represents the elevation of a culture-bound historical orientation to a universal principle.

The psychology of self-interest puts a severe strain on restraint, the central element of capitalism. The utilitarian psychology of Jeremy Bentham and John Stuart Mill heighteed the status of self-interest even more, for they said the basic individual propensity is to seek pleasure and avoid pain (though pleasure is defined as long-run pleasure not immediate satisfaction). The direction of economics, in keeping with this view of human subjectivity, turned from valuing labor to valuing the production of goods. This change in view made the crack in the door that changed the word "goods" into the word "commodities." Notice how rapidly far away we have gotten from concern with the world in this example of the historical dynamic of forgetfulness.

Neoclassical economics, whose founder was the British economist Alfred Marshall, the originator of microeconomics, introduced efficiency as the center of a psychology needed to accommodate pleasure. Once pleasure is introduced as the purpose of economics the danger arises that behavior incompatible with economy will surface — the disinclination to work, an interest in art and sensual pleasure, a search for meaningful work. Because these are all pleasures that would move us back to contact with the world, they must be subverted. Marshall's version of Melanchthon says that it is natural for human beings to maximize monetary or consumptive gains. Opposing forces, values, and interests are balanced in such a fashion as to keep pleasure in check, and the means to this balance is the budget. Economics becomes the management of pleasure. The new psychology says that it is natural to seek more and more satisfaction by consciously, deliberately maximizing all gains at a given moment through budgeting. This position, where we are now, opens the door for consumer economics: the manipulation of goods and services through attaching them to pleasurable subjective states. It also leads to the situation in which money itself becomes a commodity to be sought after, money doing business on its own detached from any relation to the soul of the world. The psychic starvation brought about by removing soul from the world produces insatiable greed, for when the world is no longer surrounded with soul a vast emptiness intervenes that must be filled. Over the last four hundred years the world has become psychopathic — very successful, very adapted, very clever, but lacking the feeling of affliction. The reduction of soul to economic psychology has made the world sick. Now there is so much sickness to care for it may force us to forget ourselves and return to the world to recover its soul. We are provided with an opportunity to enter into a new age of the soul, a new care of the world soul.

★ ★ ★

Having exposed the way in which economics replaces psyche as the primary activity of the world, and having shown economics to be nothing more than subjective psychology, we now must attempt to relocate seeing soul even within economics, a difficult but nonetheless necessary task for simply rejecting economics would give it all the more power. If we can find soul in economics, then we should be able to find soul working in a new way in the world. We must seek a way suitable for our present world rather than turning back to soulways that were suitable for former times but are actually harmful when attempted today. We have no use for the literal reenactment of magic, shamanisms, and paganisms.

What I have described as the development of modern economics might be better named economism. Economism is bestial instinctuality, not soul, carried out at the cerebral level in which money becomes detached from the world and can be manipulated without regard to reality. Economic life, to the contrary, concerns the constant interweaving of the human soul with the soul of the world, now brought to a conscious level. What might the economic process look like viewed in this manner? Modern economics comes to the foreground of life as the mythic, imaginative, religious manner of living with the world recedes. Stated another way, as individual freedom becomes more conscious, group life becomes less so. However, as freedom strengthens so does egotism, egotism of individuals and of nations. Economics expresses this changing pattern of consciousness but also carries the seeds for a new kind of group life, a conscious community of soul with the world.

Rudolf Steiner presented a series of lectures on economy which can serve as a point of departure for returning soul to economics. His contribution involves seeing through the abstract realm of modern economy to an image of the creating forces of the body; that is, he presents economics as the creation of a new body. Once we have body we are out of the head and back into the world.

Economics, seen through soul, is truly a work of art; it is the work of shaping the soul of the world into a community of soul. Economic processes re-create the soul processes of the body at a new level, the level of constant mobile flow between individual and world. At this new level the life-forming processes of the body become the realm of production; the ever-present process of dying is re-created as the realm of consumption; and from the flow of respiratory action that continually balances life and death comes the economics of supply and demand, profit and interest. The spirit enlivening this new body is the gift economy, and the soul that makes graces and messes is money. This economics works with the world, it is the medium through which soul is again enlarged to encompass everything. Let us look then at each economic activity as the recreation of the soul activity of the body, now carried out at the community and world levels, a movement toward the soul of the world.

Modern production is the child of the division of labor. The division of labor is a step toward soul community, for within this mechanism of efficiency lies a deeper reality than more production and less cost. With division of labor no one uses for himself what he produces. What one produces is passed on to others, and what one requires must now come in turn from the community. Division of labor alters egotism. It produces the feeling that "I can no longer do anything alone." It is not meant to produce unhealthy dependency, but rather a more active feeling — "I wish to do things for others." We are still at a stage of soul development at which this sense of labor produces an unsolvable dilemma. Every wage earner is a person who provides for himself, even though the very nature of work has changed in such a manner that we all provide for others. This impossible duality, that one works for a living while in actuality one works for the benefit of others, means that one gives only so much as he wants to earn. To the extent that we fulfill the demand which the division of labor involves, providing for the good of others, we are on the path beyond economism. But to the extent that the demand is unfulfilled, to the extent there is an impulse to work for oneself, we are bound to economism. Production is a likeness of the life-forming soul processes of the body insofar as it utilizes, rather than using up, the world to care for others — insofar, that is, as it cares for the world soul.

Now, what enters in to subvert this soul making is capital. The forming of capital is a concomitant of the division of labor. Division of labor is a two-edged sword. It provides for the whole while at the same time it brings about fragmentation by separating activities into parts. As capital, the results of labor, rather than being returned to the world, can be accumulated. Such a possibility arises from the abstract dimension of division of labor, for the income from such labor is easily separated from any connection to the world. From the division of labor arises capitalism, and from capitalism comes finance. Capital, expressed as the accumulation of money, becomes a declaration of the ego no longer bound to the particularities of time and place. When capital moves to finance, economic life is on the way to destruction. Finance has nothing to do with economic life as a whole. It is an imitation or double of economic life consisting of using money to make money — all cerebral activity with no world. Finance operates out of an analogy to war and to imperialism, and thus is violent, aggressive, and if left to itself will destroy itself. The limited role of capital in the economic process is that only so much capital is accumulated as can further the economic process. Anything beyond that forms an aberration.

Price determines the healthy functioning of capital. Price comes about when the producer receives as a counter-value for his product something sufficient to enable him to satisfy the whole of his needs until he will again have completed a like product. For example, if someone makes a pair of boots, the time and material it took to make the boots is not the determining factor of price. The determining factor is the time and material it will take to make the next pair of boots.

What economics calls consumption, seen through soul, is the activity of death, now carried out at the level of the community of soul. The characteristic of goods placed in the hands of a buyer is that they are always on the way to returning to nature. Either they are eaten, in which case they are taken up decidedly by nature, or they are used up, or they deteriorate. This is the death process of the economic organism. Thus, we can begin to see that economics with soul is a living organism, and that just as in the human body, a balance must obtain between life and death. Supply and demand, profit, and interest bring about this balance.

Supply is not a separate reality from demand, but together they are like breathing in and out. Supply of goods is a demand for money and supply of money is demand for goods. Not only must there be a certain number of goods available as supply, there must also be a certain number of people able to develop a supply of money for those goods. In between the life processes of production and the death processes of consumption, there exists the rhythmic breathing of supply and demand.

A similar kind of respiration goes on in the domain of profit. If the seller alone were to profit, then in the total economic life the buyer would always be placed at a disadvantage whenever an exchange takes place. We must see that the buyer too can buy in such a manner as to make a profit. When I sell something and receive money for it, I am enabled to do more with the money than the person who gives it can do. Conversely, the other person who receives the goods must be able to do more with them than I can. When I sell something the money has a greater value in my hands than in the hands of the buyer; while in the buyer's case, the goods have greater value in his hands than in mine. That is to say, profit does not belong to the seller alone, but is a rhythmic process in which both participate.

Then, a third area in which the rhythmic process goes on is interest. If someone does something for me, I feel an obligation to do something in return. A mutuality of need is recognized. Interest is what I receive if I renounce mutuality of need; if I lend someone something and we agree that that person shall be under no obligation to lend to me, the agreement is called interest. Interest therefore constitutes one of the balancing factors between production and consumption.

What we have observed about the balancing, through rhythmic processes, of life and death in the case of the body of economics we could also observe in the case of other living organisms, the animal body for example. But there is a further distinctive factor within economics, a more or less hidden life force, a soul force that indicates something of the particular nature of this body that makes it unlike other bodies. This factor we could call the gift economy: that is, all that adds to the life of the economic body through the act of giving without seeking return. For example, all housework comes under this sign, all volunteer work, all philanthropy, and education. Gift economy is exceedingly important because the gift is always oriented toward an unknown future and is an act of giving that cannot be returned except through a like giving on the part of the recipient. A gift has an unknown future because nothing is expected in return and no specification is made concerning its outcome. The receivers of gifts are pure consumers, which seems decidedly unproductive. In relation to the future, however, the gift is the most productive element in the whole economic process. Public education serves as an example. The receivers of this gift are pure consumers; the 'investors' do not receive a known return. But from the viewpoint of the future, education transforms the whole process of future production. Why is this element present in economics? It is the element of soul that enlivens the whole body, a pure act of love within an otherwise highly determined body, a body that is alive but more or less confined like an animal in a cage.

* * *

Money, says Norman O. Brown, is the soul of the world. An extraordinary sentence! Now, we must try to see how the body of economics, a body in which we have attempted to find soul, functions in the world. Money is the functioning of this body, and it is possible to find soul when we shift from money as quantity to money as quality, from money as noun to money as verb.

To begin, money remembers. The energy, aspirations, and achievements of the ancestors of the land who stood for and brought values into the community are commemorated on each denomination of currency passing through our fingertips, greening our hopes for the future. The five dollar bill remembers Lincoln as a hero of the land. Through the currency bearing his image we are called to remember that we benefit from the heroic actions of this individual, that his sacrifices and the sacrifices of all of those living at that time make possible what we have today, that it is their energy, their soul, that moves the world today. We so readily take for granted the magic ritual of the transformation of a bit of green paper into the actualization of a desire that the background making this possible goes unnoticed. Money gives the body of economics a memory. Our first step, then, regards money as value. Money values by remembering the dead.

Money is also wealth. The word wealth means well-being; it refers not only to individuals but also to the community, the commonwealth. The wealth of money is imagined as gold. In spite of the fact that paper money has not been backed by gold since 1934, there is something permanently golden about money. What is this golden quality of greenbacks?

Gold provides, in tangible form, a small glint, a touch of immortality within the world. What else could possibly account for the greed, the raw passions, that money evokes other than its having the golden touch of immortality? But the quality of gold that money carries relates to the fact that more gold is fashioned into art, jewelry, and crafted objects than is preserved as bullion. The golden quality of money takes us into the quality of money as art. Money is an art when its golden qualities craft the things of the world. As long as money carries golden fantasies, the circulation of currency keeps the element of craft closely in touch with the things of the world. Then things, each in their own proportion, also have golden qualities — attributes of permanance, beauty, solidity, fineness, the touch of the human hand.

In 1908, before the gold standard was abandoned, Freud had already discovered that the standard of wealth had shifted from the touch of immortal splendor in the world to the lowliest place imaginable, for he declared that money was more like excrement than gold. Few paid attention to such an absurd sounding statement, but Freud was getting at some very important qualities of wealth with this metaphor. We speak of dirty money, filthy lucre, the smell of cash, holding companies, putting someone on a retainer, tight money, loose money, cash flow. Money matters have a dirty side; they take us right into the messes of money, and I for one, admire those who are not afraid to get their hands dirty. The difficulties inherent in this image of money come from holding on too tightly, from thinking that the whole point of money is to accumulate it, that control of money is a matter of training in retention. The real contribution of Freud's insight is his reconnection of money matters with the vital processes of the body, the sense that the health of the communal body depends on the choreographed movement of money.

Besides being value and wealth, money is, according to the standard definition, a medium of exchange. Imagine giving fifty cents for an apple; I reach into my wallet, purse, or pocket, give the clerk two quarters, and receive a particular apple, the one that has caught my fancy. The apple draws the quarters from my pocket as the quarters give tangible substance and particularity to my imagination. To think of this moment as spending money is to operate out of an image of money as the action of retaining and letting loose. The quantitative approach isolates the exchange and treats money not as medium but as a static thing. When money is undersood as a magical medium, the transaction can be seen as condensing a whole realm of relationships — the relationships to the store in which I stand, the clerk whom I face, the employer who paid my salary, the family budget which portioned the earnings, the desire which brought me to the store, the company which owns the store, the employees which the store retains, the produce merchant who brought the apples in, the farmer who grew the apples, the particular tree from which this apple came, the earth from which the tree sprouted, the rain which moistened the tree, the clouds which shaded it, and the sun which reddened the apple. We are what we purchase; that can be as narrow as greedy functionaries or as broad as guardians of the earth.

* * *

Let us summarize our progress in this intricate and somewhat abstract story of the relation of economics, money, and the soul of the world. Our object has been to find the lost soul of the world in the abstract world of economics. We have traced how subjective psychology acting as modern economics has covered the world so that soul can no longer be seen in it. But we have been able to see soul in economics itself, to see the impulse toward making a community of soul in which individuals and world cohere in a constant recreating of the whole. And we have looked at money as having active qualities useful for recreating the body of the world as soul. Here is a story reported in the August 16, 1961 edition of the *Louisville Courier:*

> More than $150,000 in cash and securities was unearthed Tuesday in the Yorkville district apartment of an eccentric who piled about him the accumulated trash and tokens of year upon year of solitude. Amid the debris were faded reminders of life in New York half a century ago.
>
> George Aichele, 73, was found dead Monday of natural causes. It took police all night to ferret out and count $47,000 in cash in the five-room flat, including $500 and $1000 bills casually tucked amid rubbish.
>
> More than 80 bank books were also turned up, noting deposits of more than $112,000. Some of the deposits, of only $10 were made, a friend said, because Aichele coveted the minor gifts with which banks encouraged new depositors.
>
> Aichele was an incredible hoarder. He even wrapped a single penny and tucked it away with a notation he had found it outside his 66th Street apartment.
>
> "In the living room the junk was piled 5 feet high," said Patrolman James Pyne, first to enter the apartment after Aichele's lawyer missed the old bachelor for many days. There were razors and blades, newspapers and magazines dated at the turn of the century, unopened cases of liquor, phonograph records, thousands of packs of safety matches, dozens of wedding bands and diamond rings, a carton of more than 100 harmonicas, a bird cage, a zither. Aichele was a recluse as far as his home was concerned. No one but himself was known to have set foot inside it since a brother with whom he lived died 13 years ago. This brother, John, presumably took part in the hoarding since much of the trash accumulated antedated his death in 1947. Another brother, Henry, a bank

executive, died in 1956, also amid rubbish accumulated in his home. It took six months to clear it out. The brothers inherited money from their father, Charles, who made a fortune in Manhattan real estate.

This story condenses what I have had to tell of economics and money and indicates the importance of an imagination of money for the present world. Stories of misers are far less frequent than they used to be. In our time, there is no necessity for misers — they have all been converted into consumers. Both are caught by the attempt to take the whole world into their home and to possess it. Each of the senses of economics and money that we have brought forth, when pervaded with the fantasy of accumulation, turn the world into a heap of trash. Memories are then hoarded; wealth is hoarded; the medium of exchange is hoarded. To possess the world in such a manner is to live in total isolation from the world. The whole point of economics and money apparently has little to do with possession, for when possession dominates disintegration follows. The miser and the consumer alike are fraught with insecurity because they have lost connection with the soul of the world, and this insecurity is experienced as the fear of not having a future. A further observation to be made concerning the report of the demise of the miser is that the household was completely lacking in order, it had all receded back into chaos. For the consumer, it is the household of the world that is completely lacking in order, the cosmos having regressed to chaos, because the order of imagination is lacking. Possessing money, wealth, makes the world inactive, dead. Money without a future is the world falling apart, reverting to mere physical being. When money acts, it looks forward to rearrangements of the world. Such rearrangements ought not to be confused with progress, for progress is but one version of the order of things. Money changes the world in an endless variety of ways, ways that represent the constant refiguring of the soul of the world. But for money to have this effect, attention must be focused on the soul of the world, not on money. When the focus is money, the body of the world is reduced to materiality, producing great fear. Take Howard Hughes, an archetypal hoarder of money. There was no life in him, no connection to the creative element, in spite of all he accomplished. He was drawn to beautiful women but none of his relationships resulted in a creative union. He had no children he could claim, but a lot of consumers are around trying to claim him as father. He saw women as sources of income; he introduced sex into film with the production of the famous scene of bosomy Jane Russell sitting in the hay.

Howard was as tight with the excrements of his body as he was with his money. He developed a severe phobia of germs. He would not eat from silverware; those attending him had to wear surgical gloves. He would not touch anything except with a kleenex in his hand. He would not allow his fingernails to be cut, nor his hair, and suffered chronic constipation. When economics and money become the world, the soul of the world decays and returns to mere matter. The point of money is to make soul not money.

Using money to make money, I have indicated, constitutes the realm of finance; and finance seems to have nothing to do with soul. However, unless this element of economics, too, can be taken into soul it will never be possible to get beyond economism. As an image of soul within finance I turn to the recent popular film, *Die Hard.* This film has certainly not been evaluated as profound. On the surface it seems to be one more bloody, violent, cops and robbers story. I think, however, that it is an allegory of finance. A group of terrorists take over the headquarters of the Makamuto Corporation in Los Angeles. The terrorists shoot the CEO of the corporation in the head and proceed to break in the vault, located on the top floor of the skyscraper. The group issues a number of absurd political demands to make themselves seem like legitimate terrorists, and to give them time for the takeover of some billion dollars in securities that are held in the vault. Already, we

can see that this is more than a movie about terrorism. We
have a huge amount of accumulated capital in the hands of
a Japanese corporation. We have what seems to be a
terrorist takeover, not unlike a corporate takeover of stock;
in actuality the terrorists are working for no other cause
than themselves. They are no more than robbers; but to
those not involved it seems to be a political situation that
can be negotiated. The vault is no ordinary vault; it is
elaborately protected by various computer mechanisms,
and breaking into the vault involves much calculation and
cunning. And when they finally do get into the vault, not
only is it filled with accumulated capital, but also some of
the most rare and wonderful treasures of Japan — ritual
swords, art works, and priest's robes. Capital has taken its
place alongside of divine power itself, held in the holy of
holies.

The hero is a New York policeman who had come to
Los Angeles to visit his wife, the chief lieutenant of the
corporation CEO. The hero and this woman are in the
midst of deciding whether to remain together, an image of
the fragmentation of past values brought about through
capital. The hero arrives at the corporation headquarters as
the workers are having a Christmas party, and happens to
be in the bathroom when the terrorists invade. That the
story takes place at Christmas is an indication that the hero
is not an ordinary hero, although at first he seems to be as
he sets about cleverly eliminating the terrorists one by one,
employing their own tactics and weapons to do so. During
the numerous battles that take place, however, the hero,
who is barefoot throughout, must make an escape from
gunfire by walking through shattered glass. A large piece of
glass lodges in his foot, a most significant image. Our limbs
are the expression of our will; through them we move
about, reach out, take, hold onto, step over others, or
receive. Our hero has a wound of the will, so his actions
cannot be seen as pure heroic will against the bad guys. His
presence is necessary to their downfall, but is not the real

cause of it. We see in the film that another force is operating that is more powerful than direct heroic action.

Throughout the internal battle in the corporation head-quarters, in which the whole inside of the skyscraper is destroyed by fire, the hero has one connection with the outside world. The blundering police, FBI, and tactical squad attack the building from the outside. These collective forces of regulation cannot penetrate the building. The institution of finance cannot be handled by outside regulation. The hero maintains radio contact with one black policeman, with whom, through communication, he establishes a close and loving friendship. This friendship with an unknown person who becomes a brother is the force that brings downfall to the terrorists. It is an image of true community, of giving to one another.

The final image of the film portrays the struggle between the hero and the head of the terrorist group. The political demands of the terrorists were all fabricated; all along the terrorists were only interested in the capital, and were fully willing to destroy anything to get at it. When the two figures, the hero and the lead terrorist, meet, a fight ensues, and the terrorist goes plunging through a window of the skyscraper toward his death, holding a bag of securities. The securities go flying ephemerally through the sky, showing forth their unreality to the world. This terrorism is nothing other than finance destroying itself. Within the darkness of finance, however, if my reading of this film is correct, lies the possibility of the formation of a community of soul. Community is an ideal; we actually know little concerning its reality. The reality itself will appear out of the darkness, from the least expected of places — not from the system, not from the laws, not from politics, but from the offer of an unknown helping hand from the world. Will we be able to perceive through soul and capitalize on that moment?

Letter VI

Technology

DEAR FRIEND,

Technology seems to be the ultimate enemy of soul. When we speak of technology today we automatically think of electronic technology, so to pit technology against soul is the same as setting up the opposition of soul and electricity; they seem to have nothing to do with each other. So, we are faced with a large task, the task first of seeing how this opposition arises and what it entails, and then seeing how it might be possible to recover an element of soul in technology.

Techne refers to making or doing, and *logos* to knowing. Thus, *technology* concerns the kind of knowing involved in doing, and belongs to every act of making. The potter and the artist, for example, employ technology; they know what they are doing, and without the sense of technology any consideration of art is pure romanticism. With electronic technology, however, a difficulty arises, for here doing is ahead of knowing due to the fact that, as we shall see, we really do not know the nature of electricity but nevertheless go ahead and use it for the development of a technical world. A similar difficulty arises with the use of nuclear energy. We do not know what forces are at play, but we go ahead and make use of them anyway. Now, the immediate response may be that our most sophisticated knowledge lies in these two realms of electricity and nuclear physics. However, this "knowledge" is all theoretical and involves application of views of reality that function contrary to the way we actually experience the world.

This knowledge, when viewed in terms of its results, in fact seems to be knowledge of a fantasy world, justified through the proposition that the purpose of technology is to improve the human situation. We shall have to examine this situation in some detail, for it constitutes not just an addition or supplement to the world, but an entirely new reordering of the world by being forgetful of the actual world and imposing on it an alien form.

Marshall McCluhan got closer than anyone else to understanding the true character of technology, and he did so by beginning with myth. He read the myth of Narcissus as an image of technology. Narcissus, you will remember, is an adolescent, pride-filled individual loved by Echo, the nymph who through certain circumstances has been brought to a condition in which she can only repeat the last words of each sentence she hears — that is the extent of her voice. Thus, if she hears someone say, "I love you," she could only repeat, "love you." Well, Narcissus will have nothing to do with her and she wastes away; only her voice remains. We can already see the suitability of the relation of Narcissus and Echo, for any statement Narcissus might make about the world is echoed back as a Narcissistic command from the world — "I love you" comes back as "Love you."

Narcissus, we hear in the story, comes to a clear pool and therein sees an image, which he does not know to be himself, and he falls in love with this image of himself, which we can also take as a further manifestation of Echo:

> While he seeks to slake his thirst another thirst springs up, and while he drinks he is smitten by the sight of the beautiful form he sees. He loves an unsubstantial hope and thinks that substance which is only shadow.

Narcissus wastes away in longing for the unsubstantial shadow; a flower is left, "its yellow center girt with white petals."

McCluhan reads this myth as a story about technology, through which we fall in love with a shadowy replica or imitation of ourselves, exteriorized and echoing through the world. The exteriorized self lacks the substantiality of body, though it offers the shadowy hope of complete satisfaction. Technology then concerns the extension of ourselves into the world without the knowledge that this is happening. For example, with mechanical technology, parts of the body are extended into the world. The wheel is both an extension and an acceleration of walking. We, however, are unable to cope with the acceleration — it disturbs the senses. This disturbance is handled by anesthetizing the body, we begin to lose the immediate sense of the body. With electronic technology, the brain is exteriorized into the world, resulting in the autoamputation of thinking, and we enter the age of information which comes to imitate thought. And along with the imitation, or double of thought, comes the hope that this dummy thought will produce complete satisfaction.

We can begin to see through electronic technology when we are able to feel that its naive hope resembles to a very large extent the same experience as the longing for the past; that is to say, the technological imagination touches upon the same psychic domain as nostalgia; they both involve fantasies of infantilism. The memory of being unconscious, fully immersed in the world, and completely taken care of is the same as the hope for a future world in which technology will provide these same benefits. That is to say, technology, when enacted without conscious knowledge of what is involved, is not progress but regression. Finding the soul of technology requires that this confusion be clarified, this false hope abandoned, in order to diminish an inflated view of what technology is about and to locate its own limited domain.

* * *

Deflating the hope of technology by showing that it is
an imagination of primitivism takes us to the realm of
electricity as the important dimension of modern technical
achievement, electricity as that which allows doing to get
ahead of knowing. Electricity removes us from the particularity of the world. For example, without electricity, power
needs are supplied in relation to a defined environment.
Water, for example, can supply the power to grind the
wheat of a region. But with electric power, which this water
power can help create, this force is no longer limited to the
particular region, but can be realized anywhere, and without limitation. The result of this abstraction is that production becomes greater than need. A movement toward
equality of consumption also results. When powered by
water, wheat products are more plentiful in some places,
less in others. When powered by electricity, these same
products are more equally available to everyone. This
movement toward equality of consumption, however, produces the false hope that all our needs can be satisfied
through the development of technology — here we have
that narcissistic longing. The crucial question is what is
lost or forgotten when we become filled with the shadowy
hope that technology, not the world, will give us what we
need? In order to address this question we shall have to
explore something of the nature of electricity, and here the
work of Ernst Lehrs provides an invaluable source for real
thinking about electricity.

The first electrical machine was invented in the eighteenth century by a German, Guericke, who was also the
inventor of the air pump. His discovery opened the way for
the discovery that electricity could be transmitted from one
place to another. Guericke saw some similarity between air
and electricity, and that similarity is movement. He tapped
into a remarkable region through his vision, the region of
dynamic action. Whereas previously one had to look to the
world to perceive everything in movement, movement
being basic to the life of all of nature, the soul of the world
requiring constant refiguration — now, movement could do

business on its own. The early experimenters in electricity were not in the least interested in practical applications; they were really interested in the soul of the world, and they thought that they had found the essence of this soul in pure dynamics, most clearly with electricity. The history of the development of electricity into something practical is the history of accidents; the workers in this field did not know what they were doing. Galvani, the discoverer of the electrical charge, was a biologist tinkering with electricity; his interest was in what animated life. You may already know the story of how he accidentally discovered that frog legs could be made to move by touching them with two bits of different metals. He thought he had discovered the life force, that the movement he saw came from within the dead frog's limbs, not from the outside. Thereafter, Volta discovered how to produce a continuous current by immersing a zinc and copper bar in a corroding fluid — the battery was created. Then the Dane, Oersted, accidentally discovered that a magnetic force accompanies an electrical current in a direction at right angles to the current. He had just finished presenting a lecture and demonstration that showed electricity and magnetism were not related and had unknowingly left a compass near one of his wires, when he happened to notice the compass was affected by the current when placed at a certain angle. These accidental discoveries were necessary steps toward the successful transmission of current, and as well toward inventions such as the motor. But each step of the way, doing was ahead of knowing. William Crooks, the inventor of the cathode ray tube, was interested in trying to contact his dead brother and often attended seances where misty fog and flashing lights were said to be appearances of the departed. He was experimenting with the effects of electricity on gases enclosed in a tube and noticed that the effect was similar to those observed in seances. He thought he had discovered a means to communicate with the dead. Roentgen accidentally discovered x-rays when he left a cathode ray tube near a key that he had left on a photographic plate and found a shadowy picture of the key left on the plate when he developed it. This led to the discoveries of Becquerel and the Curies.

Now, all of these accidents indicate that in electricity we are dealing with an unknown force. The presently predominant theories of electricity concern how it functions, not what it is. And the fascination with electricity contains a strong element of the feeling that the soul of the world has been captured and that it is thus now possible to construct a new world. There is some truth to this: electricity does make possible the construction of a shadowy, imitation world. Television is a prime instance of such creation. We think we see a picture when we look at television, but there is nothing there but a rapidly moving series of dots and a field between screen and viewer. Together, the screen and the viewer make an image of a world that is a shadowy imitation of the actual world, an image devoid of feeling and substance. If television damages the soul it is not because of the content, but because of the medium — because we do not realize that it is a momentary, synthetic world. This forgetfulness allows for the possibility of viewing the most horrible events without feeling their reality, because in the imitation world there is no reality to be felt.

If we are to reduce the illusory power of electronic technology, we must dispel the illusion in the claim that extraordinary benefits are at hand as we enter the information age. We must expose the deception lying in the belief that everything will improve as we enter into an imitation world without soul, body, and substance. Let us look at this belief. Television teaches how to see the world in simplistic terms. It is like a comic book of the world in which all matters are treated equally, the same things presented over and over again, in which the actions presented have no permanent consequences, and wherein all events are presented as trivia with a confusion between what is real and what is not. It is the same with video games, except that here the user becomes an active participant in the shadowy world, enabled to act with violence and destructiveness

without consequence, receiving a training in disassocia-
tion. Computers treat the world as a series of problems that
can be broken down into series of simpler subproblems,
leading to a view of the world as something that can be
solved, not transformed. Computers reduce thinking to one
dimension while other dimensions of thought and imagination lose reality. When the claim for the benefits of the
information age is put forth, what is being stated is that
with electronic technology a new soul of the world is being
formed. This is true — it is the psychopathic soul.

Psychopathy is a kind of programming in life, a learning
how to "de-bug" life. The psychopath does everything
effortlessly, freely, without any sense of inhibition, restraint, or suppression. Nothing of the world makes a claim
on the soul of the psychopath. Cheating, lying, saying one
thing and doing just the opposite without the least concern,
changing a position from one moment to the next in order
to satisfy the situation, the psychopath is always a winner.
Psychopathy: appearing better than one actually is; suc-
cessfully gliding along the surface, intelligently, but without insight; passing through the world without being emo-
tionally moved, without feelings of the heart, only feelings
programmed to suit the situation. Psychopathy constantly
assures that everything works smoothly, efficiently, always
to one's advantage. Everything is a game: feelings, emotions, courtesy, love, sympathy, care — the psychopath can
imitate any form of behavior without it going through the
heart.

The resulting world can best be described as the world
of *Bladerunner*. In this film the city of Los Angeles is
pictured in the not too distant future. The image of that
city ought to strike horror in our hearts. The city is in ruins.
So much pollution fills the air that it is constantly raining.
Most of the people have left the planet; only those with
defects are left behind. Most of the buildings are abandoned
as if some surge of overdevelopment by speculators had not
borne fruit. Garbage collects everywhere. Seamy characters
roam the streets. Layered on top of this image lies a world

of technological perfection. Automatic air-lock doors open and close along the street. A huge dirigible passes over the city periodically, with neon signs advertising products. Police patrol the ruins in electronic airships. Lights, electronic gadgets, computers of every sort populate this city. We are presented a massive image of the making of a new world soul.

The main character of the film has the task of searching out a group of genetically engineered creatures who look exactly like human beings, except that they are technically perfect — they are brilliant, have incredible athletic bodies, and are extremely violent, seeing no reason whatsoever to refrain from killing those who block their psychopathic wishes. Such are the accomplishments of the information age. But wait, there is an important twist to the film. Our hero falls in love with one of the genetically engineered women, and she with him. She was constructed with the memory implant from another person, and seems to have feelings. This image is important for it opens a door that we must pass through. We have distilled the world of electronic technology to what it seems to be actually about; is it now possible to find soul there? The film in its own way says yes. Concentrating on one aspect of the technical world, the computer, I want to look again at technology rid of its impossible hopes, hoping to see through it to soul.

* * *

Things have their own psychology. The tiresome foray of psychology into the realm of individual human affairs has sidetracked us from giving attention to the work of soul in the world, trapping it for several centuries in the black box of subjectivity. The computer: what kind of thing is it? It is, after all, part of the world, and the compelling task before us is to find its soul by seeing through opinions, reactions, and judgments, through what we fear, desire, and wish and hope for, through the enthusiasms of technologists and the disgust of humanists — in order to let the computer speak for itself. The hands-on experts are not able to perceive the soul because they have come under its possession, and drunk with enthusiasm they are driven by it as if by a god or a daemonic force. Timothy Leary has recently commented from afar and on high that the video game was the LSD of the 80s; the computer, then, is the cocaine of the 90s. How does the computer figure into the ancient and everlasting questions of birth, death, life, love, hope, community, history, and a concern for all we speak of as soul?

First, it is necessary to eliminate a direction in which the use of computers, I believe, would obscure soul completely. This direction is one in which we would all be turned into computer programmers. Such a move is at hand not only through teaching children computer programming in the schools, but even more in proposals that programming replace the school curriculum. Seymour Papert, professor of education at MIT, has invented a system of programming called LOGO, in effect a new system of education. In this system the child is not presented with subject matter of any sort. Rather, whatever the child is to learn comes about by the child inventing it on the computer. For example, a child would no longer learn grammar. The subject would be replaced by the programming of a general structure, such as the structure of a poem, which is filled with words selected from a random list. The student inserts various words into the general structure until an error-free poem is produced, that is, one in which each part of grammar is perfect. The aim is to allow a child to bypass grammar because grammar is not interesting; instead the child can feel like a poet by writing a poem while incidentally, effortlessly, learning the parts of speech.

The argument in fact is quite persuasive. When we learned to talk in our early years none of us did so by studying vocabulary and the parts of speech. We would say something and then perhaps be told that we had used an incorrect word or that we had used a word in the wrong place. Gradually we learned to speak, more or less correctly. Now, what is the difference between that kind of learning and the learning proposed by programming? Most obviously, learning how to talk occurs in the context of a family, a community, and with the mediation of all the senses. Remove the family or community or put aside the senses from the act of learning and soul is removed. If one learned through programming the result would be the formation of the psychopath — all skill and no soul. So, in trying to find the soul of the computer, we must focus not on its uses and misuses, but we must take the larger view concerning how it figures into culture. Programming is an interim, a brief interlude that concerns fascination with a narrow mentality. This interlude is one, however, in which all can be lost if culture loses its sensibility.

I want to propose that the computer is not just another technological device contributing to the mechanization of the world, but is in fact the culmination of the mechanized world, the consummate result of that world, the signal for the end of that world. Joseph Weizenbaum has a brilliant insight when he says that the computer is not just another tool, just as a clock is not another tool. The clock changed our whole way of organizing experience. The computer is an invention of similar import. With the movement to mechanization the opportunity to rediscover soul was present but was not followed. With the movement to electronic technology another opportunity to rediscover soul is presented. Let me show, first, where the opportunity for recovering soul existed in the transition to mechanization, and then perhaps we can see where it might be found in the movement toward electronic technology. In 1783 Jacques de Vaucanson submitted to the Paris Academy of Science a mechanical duck. It could wade and swim. Its wings imitated nature in every way. It would move its head, quack, and pick up grain. A mechanism inside the duck ground up the grain and caused its exit from the body much as a natural movement. What connects this little historical vignette with our concern for the computer is that what was not seen in the movement to mechanization is that mechanization is sheer play. That is to say, what allowed the making of the mechanical duck was the perception of play in the world. It is, I believe, a wrong direction, and a direction that obscures soul, to make a mechanism and then say, well, you see, the world is a mechanism which we can imitate. What is missed is that the original perception was not of a mechanism but of play. The soul of the world plays.

Now, to gain a new opportunity for recovering the world soul, let us look at the computer from this angle. The story begins on June 18, 1623, with the birth of Blaise Pascal, who is credited with the invention of the modern calculator, a predecessor to the computer. I am not interested so much in the story of Pascal; rather, I intend to read some of the psychically relevant events of this life as the soul of the computer telling its myth. One of the primary ways things speak is through the lives of people. We mistakenly hear only the biography of the individual, missing the soul biography of the thing.

Pascal was born in a time of radical cultural uncertainty. It is the time of the publication of Cervantes' *Don Quixote*, which represents a nostalgia for the world as whole; and it was the time of the major work of Descartes, signaling a distrust of the appearance of things, and of the birth of Newton, hailing a serious mechanistic cosmos. It was a time of spiritual exhaustion; religious conviction was dissipated.

Pascal suffered a birth defect by which he was condemned to a lifetime of severe headaches. There are two bones in the skull of every baby which should knit up in the early weeks of life. In Pascal's case the bones never joined. It is as if he was never fully contained within the body, as if he suffered an open and direct connection linking his brain with the surrounding world. In a sense, his physiology is a negation of Descartes, for a brain in such close sensitive connection with the world at large defies the confinement of subjectivity that was proclaimed by Descartes. In ancient times such a condition would certainly have been taken as the mark of a spiritual gift.

There is another detail that makes Pascal's life of mythical import, the death of his mother in his childhood. In itself that may not be unusual, except for the fact that his father arranged his own life in such a manner as to be father, mother, and tutor to his child. And in the education of his child Etienne was most extraordinary. The father's own bent for mathematics coupled with the son's eagerness from the earliest age to know the reasons for all things meant that Pascal never learned content without going through its reasons. One story has it that at the age of twelve Pascal rediscovered the whole of Euclid independently, up to the thirty-second proposition of the first book. He seemed unlimited in the joy of learning how to learn.

Pascal, master mathematician at the age of sixteen, astounded his contemporaries with his work on conic sections. He isolated and proved the peculiar property common to all conic sectional curves, namely, that if any six points on the curve be joined up and the sides of the resulting hexagon be produced beyond the curve, the three pairs of opposite sides will meet at three points that are in a straight line. There are three observations to be made here. First, Pascal had a passion for the concrete and the actual. While Descartes, for example, was brilliant at devising algebraic methods to solve all geometric problems, Pascal insisted on the diagram. He remained nearer to the tangible facts. Second, Pascal's genius lay more in recombining and seeing things in new ways than in sheer invention. Much of the work on conic sections had already been devised by Descartes. This approach is also characteristic of most of Pascal's work — he was possessed of a genius for synthesis. Third, his work with conic sections revealed a peculiar feeling about infinity; in the essay on conic sections two of the curves involved go off to infinity, and all three of them involve infinitesimals in the calculations to which they give rise. Mystically, this feeling for infinity governed all his thoughts about human nature also, and brought him to a point at which he saw all things through the vision of eternity.

We must mention the invention of the calculator itself, which occurred in 1640. It was an invention made as a gift for his father who was working as a tax assessor. His father often complained to his son that his calculations kept him up nightly until two o'clock. Blaise conceived of a mechanism that could add, subtract, multiply, and divide, including a device for carrying the correct digits from one column to the next, and another for recording the results. We are so accustomed to such devices that it is difficult to realize the import of this invention; I do not mean the practical import, but the kind of soul that could imagine such a thing. It is one that is able to locate a purely spiritual activity within a mechanistic universe. I do not locate this wonder so much with the individual Pascal, but with the soul of the world that played through the open head of this person.

In 1645 a new interest came to Pascal which would occupy his attention for years, a concern for the void. It came to him, of course, in the form of an interest in a phenomenon in the world; but the word *void* carried all the mythic connotations of the great abyss out of which all creation comes. The physical phenomenon was presented by a scientist, Pierre Petit. The open end of a four-foot tube completely filled with mercury was inverted into a vessel also containing mercury. The mercury in the tube partly descended, leaving at the top of the tube a space, apparently completely empty. The question posed was what is the nature of the peculiar emptiness? The most frequent and accepted explanation of the day was that the phenomenon was occasioned by "spirits of the air." After later experiments, this mythic language was converted into the emerging mechanistic language — it was a phenomenon of air pressure.

Pascal, seer through the eyes of infinity, saw deeply into this phenomenon. It was a turning point in his life. He began to remove himself from experimentation and from mathematics and to be more concerned with the divine. It was as if he saw in the phenomenon of the rising mercury that the mind could go only so far before confronting an absolute void, a void that fascinated Pascal more than the mind itself. On the evening of September 23, 1654, Pascal was in the middle of studying the seventeenth chapter of St. John's Gospel where Christ prepares himself for the last sacrifice. Pascal was suffering severely from headache and prayed: "Open my heart Lord . . . the idea of the world in my heart is so engraved that your idea is no longer recognizable . . . let me find you inside myself since I cannot look for you in the world because of my weakness . . . enter into my heart and soul." When he so thought and prayed a visionary state came upon him, lasting from half past ten in the evening until half past twelve. Such was the conversion of Pascal. After this moment Pascal relinquished his active work in science. He was no longer inflated with what science might be able to do.

The myth of the computer, told through the more mythic aspects of the biography of Pascal, repeats itself now. Recognizing such a pattern lets the soul of the computer show forth. The computer brings great expectations. But these expectations must be seen against the background of our cultural disintegration which is not unlike that of the 1600s. And our situation with the computer must be seen against the background of the mentality of Descartes, whose position held sway over that of Pascal. The position of Descartes led to the reign of subjectivity and the degradation of the soul of the world, setting the conditions for the fragmentation of the world. So, if the computer carries our hopes of the future, we must be clear about the nature of our desires. We can hope to extend the vision of Descartes. The computer, then, constitutes a technological device for the mastery of the world of things, removing us even further from direct contact with the soul of the world. Or we can hope that the computer will radically alter our outlook, that we can see through the computer to the void and that in this void can be seen the world soul.

Pascal's invention of the calculator relieved the labors of the father; it allowed the father to sleep, perchance to dream. The calculator thus serves as an image of cultural transformation. The computer frees us from the routines of labor, allows the genius to play; but it also signals the loss of certainty that the father structure embodies, and it moves us into the world of chance and probability. This is particularly so because the freeing from the complaining father in the Pascal story does not lead to an embrace by the mother, for Pascal's mother is absent. The play of the computer is not the delight of play protected by the warmth of the mother, but is a kind of playfulness in an empty void. That is, the age of the computer lacks the certainties of the father spirit and also the warmth of the protectiveness of benevolent mother.

The greatest promise of the computer, then, is that it will show us that we are lost. But it can also show us what to do when lost, that the most meaningful activity when lost is the activity of play, which is also allowing the soul of the world its play. In the case of Pascal the combination of spiritual longing with play led to conversion. We need not take this to mean that computers will lead us all to be born again Christians, but through computers the possibility of a turnaround, of a metanoia, does exist. The computer's play, by freeing us from the labors of the mechanistic world, by freeing us from investing our spirit in the production of commodities, allows perhaps the last possibility of paying attention to the world. I want to call this the Pascal option. If we opt, on the other hand, for Descartes, the computer signals a beginning of the final and complete loss of the presence of the world soul.

* * *

With electronic technology an acceleration of the world occurs, and with acceleration comes the loss of qualities;

color, texture, luster are replaced by mathematical logic. Technology itself, when looked at as a world phenomenon, can be seen as speed. The value of speed replaces the qualities of the world. But, given these two polarities alone — speed and quality — I like to think quality will win out. There must be another aspect to electronic technology that weights the present world in this direction.

Electricity deals with the forces of creation; this can be seen in the natural electrical phenomenon of lightning. Lightning does not just accompany clouds and rain, but constitutes the very creation of water. Mechanistic explanations of rain hold simply that water evaporates from the earth, rises to a certain level, accumulates in clouds, and falls again. Luke Howard, an investigator of clouds working at the time of Goethe and employing a method of observation similar to that of Goethe, the method of seeing what is actually present rather than inventing theories, observed the following: going from the clouds closest to earth to those furthest away, there exist five types of clouds — nimbus, stratus, cumulus, cirrus, and the heat mantle, the uppermost state. Evaporation occurs to the point at which water no longer exists. This heat mantle then begins new formations — it is not a question of condensation but of new formations. At the moment of lightning there occurs the creation of water. From these observations we are now able to say that the power of electric technology derives not only from its speed but also from its felt capacity to create a world. The change in imagination from Michelangelo to Benjamin Franklin has given man the capability of creating an imitation world. That is not all; to carry out this illusion of creation, technology must also harness magnetism.

Magnetism is a natural phenomenon of the earth, connected with the poles. The earth's magnetic field is so arranged that the majority of land mass lies to the north, constituting the negative (dry) magnetic pole. The majority of the water mass lies to the south, forming the positive (wet) magnetic pole. This polarity keeps the earth in balance. All electrical phenomena of technology require positive-negative polarity. Harnessing this polarity must involve a disturbance of the balance. Thus, speed is only the outward sign of the creation of an imitation world. Through electricity and magnetism the forces of creation are grasped by human hands that do not know what they are doing.

The manic urge to create a technological world arises when soul can no longer be felt as a creative force in the world. Strengthening the forces of soul, of imagination, can gradually bring about a balance — a balance that does not require abandoning technology but considerably diminishes the fantasies invested in it. When soul creates, it does so in terms of qualities, and only as its action is severely impaired are we prone to take speed as a substitute for soul making.

LETTER VII

Things

DEAR FRIEND,

The soul of the world, I believe, shows herself most immediately with the presence of everyday things. The word thing means a gathering together. Things, rather than being lifeless, inanimate matter, are gathering places of soul, which, when seen from their point of view, have the purpose of creating a world in which life takes place. It is impossible to conceive of a world without things; they shape the range of possibilities within which life occurs and determine how full or how empty human experience can be. The silent world of things carries out the task of imagining a world. In certain moments, with practice, it is actually possible to catch an immediate glimpse of the soul in things. Kathleen Raine, England's prized poet, writes of such a moment of imaginative vision:

> There have been times — or shall I say there was one unforgettable time — when I saw this world as a living being. It was a very simple event, such as might happen any day, to anyone. I was sitting alone in my room, writing at a table on which there stood a hyacinth growing in a glass. I was thinking of nothing in particular ... when before my eyes the world was changed. The hyacinth appeared in a flow of living light that was in some mysterious way not separate from me but like a part of my own being. Inner and outer were indistinguishably one. At the same time I know that I was seeing more fully what was really there. I have remembered it

always, although I have never again experienced the like.
But once is enough to know forever.

What makes such a moment of experience possible?
Such experiences, I suggest, are likely to become more
frequent as we pass from the age of Pisces into the age of
Aquarius. The so-called new age does not consist of spiritual practices oriented toward joyous journeys into the
interior of the self, but of the world presenting itself as
soul-filled. Pisces is imaged as a pair of fishes, alongside one
another, one pointing in an upward direction and the other
pointing in a downward direction. This image symbolizes
seeing through a perception of opposites, a primary opposition being between the human as the domain of the living
soul and the world the domain of dead matter. Aquarius is
pictured as the waterbearer, a woman holding a large urn, a
flow of water pouring out of the urn. The urn contains
water, and water is also pouring out of the urn. What is
inside is also outside, and in the image, it is not even
possible to say that the water pours only in the direction
out of the urn. The image may just as well be seen as water
pouring into the urn, containing within what was outside
and pouring forth the inner sense for things outside.
   That things are now perceived as inert is due in a large
measure to the discovery of the force of gravity by Newton.
The density and cohesion of matter derives from the force
of gravity. But gravity is not the only force. John Ruskin
once pointed out that Newton, in focusing on gravity,
asked and answered the easy question concerning why an
apple falls from the tree. But he never thought to ask the
infinitely more difficult question, how did the apple get up
there in the first place? There is something in the force of
the sap of a tree that goes counter to gravity. This something was well known before Newton's time and was called
levity.
   Levity is an actual force having to do with the spatial
extension of matter. The play of this force is not confined to
what the senses perceive as the boundaries of things. That

is to say, things, material things, are always reaching out beyond themselves, extending themselves as a revelation of their soul. This propensity of the material world to extend itself and not only to contract into more and more compact density forms the basis for the preparation of medicinal substances in homeopathy. A homeopathic remedy is prepared by taking a substance from the world and successively diluting it more and more with water until not a single molecule of the original substance remains; at this point of dilution, what was substance becomes a healing remedy. In the practice of homeopathy the quality of levity belonging to substances is transferred to the medium of water. Homeopathy is a process of removing the levity of a substance from its gravity, and thus is curative because it produces a like movement within the body, the movement from the gravity of disease to the levity of soul. The point of learning to give attention to things is similarly homeopathic: to free them from the deadening force of gravity through the perception of their levity, that is to say, their qualities — to see things as qualities rather than quantities.

Rather dramatic instances of levity do exist in the world, instances which do not require the kind of work of imagination in daily life which we shall see is needed to perceive the soul of ordinary things. These naturally occurring instances can alert us to the presence of the force of soul in matter. Phosphorus, for example, which is found in the roots and flowers of plants and also in the human brain, is to a high degree a substance of levity. It is a mineral substance that when exposed to air bursts into fire; that is, it does not tend toward a state of compactness but is a substance radiating beyond itself. Sulphur is more mixed, for it is a mineral substance that burns. It is a substance with nearly an equal portion of gravity and levity. Sulphur is found in the leaves of plants and in the protein substances of the body. Both phosphorus and sulphur point to a quality of the soul of things, and that quality is warmth. Because of modern physics and chemistry, heat is now considered to be not a quality but an increase in the average

distance between molecules caused by an increase in movement of the molecules. But this is not what is immediately
given; it is a mechanistic theory which has gradually
brought about the inability to perceive the soul of things.
Things formerly perceived as having the warmth of soul are
now seen as cold and inert.

That things are activities and not just inert masses
accounts for the power of all sacred places. The great
pyramid of Giza, for example. Is it just a monument, or is it
an astronomical observatory, a geographical marker, a tomb,
or a center of initiation? All such views look upon the
pyramid as an object rather than as a function, as a place in
which certain functions were perhaps performed, but essentially as a static form. We must be prepared to see the great
pyramid as an activity, as a verb rather than as a noun, an
ongoing activity between the above and the below in which
what acts above acts below and what acts below acts above.
Thus, everything about the great pyramid is in alignment
with the sun, the moon, the planets, and the fixed stars,
making it an activity of the cosmos here on earth. The great
pyramid is a great constellation of soul in the world. So is
the cathedral of Chartres; all sacred sites are great concen-
trations of the soul of the world. The soul of the world,
however, is now fragmented, dispersed, scattered into the
world of everyday things, and on our side is the concentration required for soul to makes its appearance.

* * *

What physics has done to the world through its focus on
gravity, language has done to the world through boxing in
things with the force of nouns. The soul of things is kept at
a distance as long as naming them with nouns comes
between us and their self-presentation. Noun language
veils the display of the colors, edges, curves, hardness,
softness, gloom and brightness of things. The repression of
the animation of the world is a cultural repression because
the practice of naming things as nouns has completely

invaded language and now determines what counts as significant — except for the poets. We get a glimpse of what things have to say by looking to writers who have concerned themselves with letting things speak for themselves.

Consider some lines from Gertrude Stein: "A Carafe, that is a Blind Glass." Under this title, follows: "A kind in glass and a cousin, a spectacle, and nothing strange. A single hurt color and an arrangement in a system to pointing. All this and not ordinary, nor unordered in not resembling. The difference is spreading." Here we have a thing, not abstract but very particular, a carafe seen at four in the afternoon by Gertrude Stein on a table in her house in Paris. But we do not have here a subjective account of what happened to Gertrude Stein at the moment the object appears. Rather, the thing speaks. This blind glass is one of a kind, but it has cousins, others resembling it. This glass, not clear, is a spectacle, not those one wears to see through, for it is blind, like dark glasses, which are to look at, not through, signifying a hurt. The glass carafe is at the same time an arrangement of words, a poem, ordered; even though it does not resemble anything known, unusual even as poetry. The particularity of this thing, when recognized, spreads as if an enhancement of the voice of all things.

For imagination, nouns act as verbs. A colleague of Ezra Pound, Ernest Fenollosa, found that in the written characters of Chinese all words, even nouns, act as verbs, and the characters picture such action. Things, Fenollosa says, are meeting points, terminal points, like snapshots of actions. Conversely, there is no action without things. Stein's poems are close to Chinese written characters. She was aware of this connection. One of her hieroglyphs says: "In China there is no need of China because in China china is china." Her words remind us that naming names the action of things.

If the noun hides the action of things, a symptomatic companion of noun consciousness lies in the copula "is." "Is" seems to imply a state of existence, as in "the cup is red." The red seems accidental to the cup, something added to the particular case of an abstract entity. The red-ing cup, a particular, momentary defining action, loses its soul when red and cup are made opposites linked through "is." However, within the copula, preserving itself from utter destruction, soul conceals itself. "Is" comes from the Aryan root as — to breathe. The soul life of the cup, its breath, hides between two generalities in suspended animation. "Is," Fenollosa tells us, drawn as a Chinese character, pictures "to snatch the moon with the hand." The ever changing, waxing and waning moon, the reflection of the cosmos in constant motion, when captured by the hand and arrested as "is," stops the motion of all things, hiding their levity, subjecting us to their gravity.

Jorges Luis Borges attempted once in a short story to picture a geographical place he called Tlon, where the physical world consists of a confluence of actions. In the language of such a world, he says, there are no nouns, "there are impersonal verbs qualified by monosyllabic suffixes or prefixes which have the force of verbs." In southern Tlon, there occurs no noun "moon" but a verb "to moon," or alternately, "to moonate." Speaking of the moon rising over the sea, one says in Tlon, "upward behind the onstreaming it mooned." In the northern hemisphere the prime unit of language is the monosyllabic adjective. Again, there is no word for moon. Instead, one says, "airy-clear over dark-round," or "orange-faint-of-sky." Hence language serves as an effective arrangement of the world's soul action; objects present themselves as precarious bundles of qualities attracting and repelling each other. Says Borges, "We touch a round form, see a glob of dawn-colored light, a tickle delights our mouth, and we falsely say these three heterogeneous things are one, known as an orange."

No single entity qualifies as a thing. The illusion of entities belongs to the world of production and commodities. The isolation of things from qualitative action reduces language itself to a commodity to be sold in the schools as a separating of the world into discrete disciplines, bought by students to prepare themselves to speak the world into inertness. Language, the commodity, becomes an initiation into the slave market in which the soul of things is bought and sold. To release things requires the emancipation of words into language that can be as changeable as the swirling forces of soul in the world, for a moment the words coming close enough together to speak a thing, then quickly dispersing to form new alliances and antagonisms. Borges wanted language to be up to such action. "Why not create a word, one single word, for our simultaneous perception of cattle bells ringing in the afternoon and the sunset in the distance? "

The intermingling of things as soul with the individual soul makes a congenial world of soul. Francis Ponge, poet of things, concentrated on this relation, and from the beginning of the twenties was drawn to the side of things, making proems that speak an animated world. One such example, *STOVES:*

> The animation of stoves is in inverse proportion to the clemency of the weather. But how, to these modest towers of heat, give expression to our gratitude? We who adore them as much as trunks of trees, humid radiators in summer of shadow and freshness, cannot for that embrace them. Nor can we even too much approach them without blushing . . . While they blush from the satisfaction they give us. By all their little crackling of dilation they caution and send us away. How good it is, then to half-open their door and discover their ardor: then with a sadistic burning stick stir the depths of the kaleidoscope, changing red to black and from fire to delicate gray the coal into embers, and the embers into ash. If they cool down, soon a sonorous sneezing warns you of oncoming headcold to punish your wrongs. The relations of man to his stove are quite far from being those of a lord to his valet.

The grammatical simplicity of these proems disguises the psychological effort involved in the meeting of individual and world soul. Ponge spent years writing a proem, often opposing his own inclination in choosing objects, in order to avoid seeing his own consciousness in them. With Ponge, words reenter the world. The substance of the world shapes words into itself, into things with an animation that is acceptable to them. Ponge's work exemplifies a soul work with things; working on words works on the things and works at the same time on soul. He says: "I insist upon saying that, as for me, I am of another breed, and for instance, besides all the qualities that I have in common with the rat, the lion, and the net, I hold to those that belong to the diamond, and besides, I am entirely at one with the sea and the cliff that it attacks, and with the pebble that finds itself created as a result."

Engagement with things moves our soul outside to find kinship with their soul, with who they are and what they want, moves us also outside of both terrible psychologism and terrible humanism. The former reduces the soul to what goes on inside and the latter produces nostalgic and perfectionist longings taking the place of soul making.

* * *

The poets give an orientation toward things; now for the practice. Attending to things begins with stopping — I am here following Aristotle who spoke of beauty as the arresting of motion. When consciousness ceases, things speak. The work consists, however, in stopping while remaining nonetheless fully awake and present. Kathleen Raine once made the statement that in the modern world the notion of energy has replaced the presence of beauty. Attending to things reverts energy to beauty. When we do stop for a moment, a great anxiety comes. That anxiety perhaps is the beauty drained from the world, converted into subjective energy. Stopping for just a moment to pay attention is very difficult — we may lose our energy. Subjectivity must be sacrificed to the thing, a ritual recognizing that subjectivity does not belong to us; we have gotten it from the world, and it is to be returned to where it belongs.

When we stop there is a sense of death, the sense that nothing is happening. At first there seems to be just a physical object before us. But that way of perceiving too needs to be stopped for seeing a physical object is a subjective activity. It must give way to another kind of perception — no longer looking at a thing, but being seen by it.

Stopping empties us, prepares us to be penetrated by the thing. But if stopping were a total emptying, it is entirely possible that things would kill us. I wonder whether we could stand their reality. Just imagine a moment — allowing things to be fully and completely themselves — no preconceptions, judgments, thoughts, ideas, feelings, memories to screen their full presence. Who of us could stand so much reality? The poet and the artist approach such a condition, make it an art. When things look at us, they reveal, manifest themselves to the heart. Their revelation does not take place in the form of general categories, classes, or meanings, but with utter particularity; this is the difference between objects and things. The ego knows objects. Only the heart knows things. The ego's relation to objects is one of consumption. The relation of the heart to things is one of breathing in, gasping, inspiration. Matisse understood something of this. In his 1947 work called *Jazz*, he says: "In art the truth, the real, begins only when one no longer understands — then one must present oneself with the greatest of humility, completely white, pure, candid, the brain seemingly empty, in a state of mind analogous to that of the communicant approaching the Holy Table. Of course one must have all one's accomplishments behind one and have known how to keep freshness of instinct." When understanding departs, things reveal themselves. We must go to things unarmed, without any conception, without any understanding, without intention.

In a little book, *Beauty Looks After Herself*, the British sculptor Eric Gill struggles with making things that are

more than representational, things that present the reality
they image. He was particularly concerned with sacred art;
in the midst of struggle, this statement breaks through, as
though the thing itself finally found language: "A crucifix
is not a picture of Christ on the cross, it is Christ on the
cross — Christ himself in wood or stone, as Christ himself
would be if he were made of wood or stone — a wooden
Christ or a stone Christ, not an imitation in wood or stone
of Christ made of flesh and blood."

But the world itself is full of the presence of sacred
things, ordinary things, and regardless of the processes of
shaping they have been through, the soul of the world can
be apprehended through them, if we but stop and pay
attention. What Gill does with sacred art, Louise Nevelson
does with the discarded things of the world. She collects the
simplest things from the garbage heaps of the city and
shapes them into art, an art that does no more than to honor
the presence of things. Frank O'Hara once said of the
sculpture of David Smith: "The best of the current sculp-
tures didn't make me feel I wanted to have one. They made
me feel I wanted to be one." That is what things ought to
make us feel. In the Christian cosmology the highest order
of the angels, the Seraphim, are assigned as inhabitants of
the things of the world. To be able to be a thing is to be able
to converse with the angels.

Let me multiply these examples in an attempt to shift
soul to the side of the world. Robert Edmund Jones, the
great dramatist, speaks of the imagination of light:

> But at rare moments, a strange thing happens, we are
> overcome by a realization of the livingness of light. The
> true light, the true performance-light is a radiance, a
> nimbus, a subtle elixir, wherein the characters of the
> drama may manifest themselves in their inmost reality.
> Lighting a scene consists not only in throwing light upon
> objects but in throwing light upon a subject. We have our
> choice of lighting a drama from the outside, as a specta-
> tor, or from the inside, as a part of the drama's

experience. We light the actors and the setting, it is true, but we illuminate the drama. Light, living light, reveals the drama.

Here is someone who knows something of the qualities of things and how to encourage them to reveal their soul. Here is someone who, when we meditate on his words, throws light on things.

Another instance: A psychotherapy patient attempted suicide by cutting her wrists, an unsuccessful attempt. In a therapy hour some time later she spoke of going to a jeweler to buy a bracelet partly intended to cover the scar on her wrist. At first the woman said she wanted a hollow bracelet that was gold plated. As I listened, I felt uneasy, as if she were trying to gold-plate an inner hollowness. But she went on. The jeweler, who must have been a wise person, looked into her eyes and said that would not do. And it did not seem to be the case that he was attempting to make a better sale. He said she must have a solid bracelet of gold. She showed me this thing, a delicate, finely woven stand of gold that did not cover the scar but honored it. She smiled; we both knew she no longer felt hollow. The bracelet told her.

Somewhere Francis Ponge says that it is important, in giving attention to things, that there be many things; no singulars. The world is polytheistic. Attention to singulars, he says, would turn us into mystics. Multiple attention is what is needed, a kind of shifting eye, a seeing out of the corner of the eye, for such multiplicity characterizes the soul of things; and as well shiftiness characterizes their imagination. While psychology still locates imagination within the recesses of subjectivity, the word *imagination* belongs to the side of the world. The Indo-European root of the word *imagination* refers to anything changing or inter-mittent, capable of catching and fixing one's attention. The Sanskrit root of the word refers to the ever-changing, ensnaring play of appearances. Imagination also means something fleeting, like a cloud, or that which winks or signals. To approach the multiplicity of the things of the world requires imagination because they are imagination in action — things as changeful, spellbinding, shuddering, arresting, magical, tricky, elusive, shimmering.

Things require specific but unloyal attention; they do not need to be put up on a shelf and idolized. People may need that, but things do not, for there is no need to favor one thing over another. Each has its own particularity, which comes forward in a moment of attention and then disappears. Only the romantic would hope to find one thing within which all beauty rests.

* * *

The practice of giving attention to things puts into play what many artists spend their lives pursuing; that is, one of the purposes of art is to let things speak. Van Gogh, for example, said: "The nature we see and the nature we feel, the one out there and the one in here, both must permeate each other in order to last, to live." And Cezanne: "The landscape mirrors itself, thinks itself within me . . . perhaps this is all nonsense, but it seems to me as though I myself were the subjective consciousness of this landscape. But if the artist intrudes, if he dares to interfere in the process of translation, he will only bring his own personal unimportance and insignificance into it. . . . He must silence all voices of prejudice within himself, forget, forget, make silence, be a perfect echo." Now, if one has this outlook and in addition has great talent, then one is an artist, that is to say, a maker of what is real. But it is also possible to have this outlook as the necessary mode of serving the soul of things; it is only necessary to put into question what physics, the science of things, has told us about their reality; take color, for example. Color constitutes one of the primary qualities of things. Imagine a room in which all of the things are of a single color — the things essentially disappear. Physics explains the nature of color in material objects in the following way: Why is an object red? It is red because it absorbs all the other colors and reflects only red. This is an explanation based more or less on the kind of logic which says: Why is a man stupid? Fundamentally he is stupid because he has absorbed a great deal of cleverness and radiates only stupidity. Consider a painter who wishes to make a picture of a wall. If a wall is depicted in a painting, it will not be a wall but only a representation of a wall unless the color is made inwardly luminous. The colors must shine inwardly. This artistic experience tells us that color is not merely absorbed by a lifeless, mineralized substance, but that color lives within it and emanates from it. If you paint a picture of a wall as if all colors are absorbed except the one color which is the color of the wall, the wall will not look like a wall but like a dead object. Things of color possess an inner luminosity. Light makes the colors visible, but the source of the color is within.

Since we live in a world now more like the world of physics than the world of the artist, the demand is more on us to bring out the soul qualities of things, for these qualities will not be immediately evident. We can meet this demand first by experiencing the action of the individual soul in the presence of things. Let us contemplate the way in which we see with two eyes, briefly, and not technically. Each eye has an independent vision. Two pictures are created when we look at anything. It is easy to determine this: look at an object at a little distance, and while looking, alternately close the left eye and the right eye. The picture of the object appears to jump from the left to the right of one's nose. When both eyes are open the two pictures fuse into one. The question that arises from this experiment is — what enters as a power to create one picture out of two? This can, of course, be explained by the mechanics of the eye focusing on the object. But what power directs the mechanics of the eye?

Now, when you look at a blue spot, concentrate on it for a few moments, and then close your eyes, you see a yellow spot of light. The complementary color is not seen either by the left eye or by the right eye, but is seen at the center. It is the power of this center that fuses the pictures of the left and right eyes into a whole. This is the soul, creating the complement of the color of the thing. The soul projects the complementary color. Thus, the taking in of the sense world is always accompanied by a pouring out of the soul, and the two activities together constitute seeing. This is so for all the colors of the rainbow; the complementary colors are called out from within. Meditating on individual colors is thus a practice in strengthening the powers of soul needed to bring out the soul color of things. Such meditation was one of the disciplines carried out in all of the centers of mystery wisdom. It is a discipline for the development of clairvoyance, which simply means clear vision, the complementary action of the soul of things with the individual soul. In our time, this practice need not take place in mystery centers, but rather in the full presence of the everyday world.

When we look at a blue surface that is before us, that blue is color in space and makes us feel that color is fixed, a noun rather than a verb. When we close our eyes and see yellow, that yellow is not experienced in the same way as the blue. It is more flat and seems to hover or float freely, without the sense that it is attached to anything, and it appears to move, for example to pulsate; it is mobile. In earlier ages, the outer world of color moved in this manner. This mobile world of color has ceased since about the fifteenth century, and now more is asked of us to uphold, to stand for the soul of things. But such a demand does not in any way indicate a movement toward the individual soul and a movement away from the soul of the world. For the mobile, yellow quality of soul, the blue quality of the world is required; the two together are needed to experience the soul of the world. The notion that in order to work on the world with soul we must first find our own soul remains caught in subjectivism. Without the soul of things our soul is a play of shadows in a dark cave, a prison.

* * *

The psychology of the prison is based on the removal of things. Bare walls, bars, a bed and a toilet. This kind of place would seem ideal for experiencing one's soul, a place unencumbered by the world. We think the same of the monk's cell — a cubicle of a room, with a table, a bed, and that is about all — and of the psychotherapist's office, where soul is to be confronted directly. But wherever we find the removal of things, we find diminishment of soul, soul without density, solidity, substance. Things will not let us alone; they need us.

Recently someone told me how several patients on the adolescent psychiatric ward of a local hospital became involved in a kind of epidemic of swallowing things. It started with a girl who swallowed a box of thumbtacks. This was really quite serious, and she had to be opened up to have them removed. You would think that this would be enough to stop other patients from following a similar practice. But then another patient took all the staples out of the magazines and swallowed them. Then a third swallowed the battery out of his electric watch. A fourth swallowed her pierced earrings. The doctors said that they were all suicide attempts, but not serious attempts because each of the patients reported what had been done. Then the psychiatrists saw what happened as the patients trying to get attention. But it is the things that got attention. If one walks down the ward of that hospital and pays attention to things, the ward is much like the prison and the monk's cell. Each room is barren, empty — a dresser, a bed, a curtain, and another bed. The swallowing of things is a kind of homage to things, a ritual honoring of the power of things. It is the taking in of things in the attempt to fill the absence within, to feel the sharp edge of the world. Since this series of incidents, the staff has instituted a nightly search through the rooms, checking in all the drawers, under the beds, under the mattresses — for things. The patients have played a wonderful trick on the psychiatrists. Now everyone is aware of things. Every night, for fear of deadly things lurking in the dark, the staff goes on a search to rid the ward of the daemonic creatures. The things have gotten their way. They are returning.

* * *

A discussion of the soul of things inevitably leads to doubts whether the machine-made technical things of the present world have soul value. One can look upon the things of nature and feel the presence of soul; and one can look at handcrafted objects and feel soul there; or one can look upon anything antique in nature and experience its soul. But one stops short with this sensibility when it comes to most of the things that now populate the world. I do not think ordinary things lack soul; rather, they require soul work, and they therefore are of far greater importance than those things that seem to give of their essence freely. Through work with everyday things the forces of soul can be developed, while in the case of things all agree upon as expressing soul, no work is required and little capacity develops. This difference is like the difference between eating meat and eating vegetables. Meat comes from animals that have eaten plants; the animal body has already done the work of digesting the plants, and thus a kind of predigestion has already occurred that makes meat eating easier for the human body than eating vegetables. More soul forces are required for the work of living on plants than for that of living on meat, and consequently certain soul forces atrophy on an exclusively meat diet. This is not an argument for vegetarianism because many other factors are involved; it is an illustration of the value of and need for soul work in the present age. To give attention to things that do not seem to warrant it may result in the capacity to perceive the soul of the world in its pain and pathology. Designer things, items turned superficially beautiful to induce a buyer to purchase what is not required, partake of soul pathology and appeal not to the imagination to join with them, but to the fancy. And when such fanciful things arrive home removed from the fancy rhetoric of the showroom, they quickly fade into oblivion or misuse and neglect. The things of the world offer themselves for use; when instead they are used up without attention, nothing returns to the world through their instrumentality and the soul of the world is further diminished. The task does not seem to be one of avoiding things or seeking only those with inherent soul presence, but of utilizing things with a sense of soul in order to return soul to the world.

LETTER VIII

Violence and the
Longing for Beauty

DEAR FRIEND,

The incapacity to experience the beauty of the soul of the world is not counted among known illnesses. Perhaps it is an illness so wide in scope, so pervasive, that it constitutes a normal abnormality. If there were such a syndrome, let us call it "aesthetic amnesia," a diagnostic manual might describe it in this way:

> This syndrome consists of an unresponsive disposition to beauty, a coldness of the aesthetic function, together with a culturally reinforced rationalization excluding beauty from the definition of consciousness. Cold unresponsiveness alternates with random activity lacking feeling but carrying the illusion of having functional utility. Those afflicted with the syndrome enjoy all the extremes and exaggerations of utility, an obsessiveness with the frivolous and the garish. Cold stupor alternates with feverish searching for and purchasing of grotesque decorative household items.
>
> Generally, the childhood experience of the patient consists of being surrounded with people equating worth with function. Often, the child's mother has a predilection for television game shows in which avocado-colored refrigerators, wood-styled formica-topped dishwashers, and purple vinyl-topped automobiles are given away as prizes. The father usually concentrates on becoming a more aggressive salesman, manager, accountant, or on more technically oriented work.

The school experience of the patient generally consists of an absence of art of any form. Later in life beauty
is regarded as incongruity of form. Patients often report
fond memories of shopping in centers built like Medieval
castles or Nantucket fishing villages. Many patients
report a trip to Disneyland as their most significant
memory.

Diagnosis: this condition is not amenable to therapy.
Hospitalization is required when the cyclic rhythm of
cold stupor with random activity quite suddenly erupts
into unexplainable violence.

Having concocted the illness as a fiction, I was drawn
back into the psychiatric literature for another look. There,
almost invisible in its lack of import, I found a description
of a psychopathology known as "cyclothymia." Though not
explicitly related to beauty, cyclothymia closely resembles
the form of the illness just described. Particularly the
alteration between stupor and activity, interspersed with
anger. The French called the illness *folie circulaire*, and it
was described by Pierre Janet in his two-volume work
Psychological Healing, published in 1925. Sufferers experience a circular rhythm of mood, a cycle of mild depression
or stupor and random bodily activity, interspersed with
anger. A recent text says that cyclothymia is like hysteria,
but is much more prevalent in men as hysteria is more
prevalent in women. Janet distinguished *folie circulaire*
from both hysteria and manic-depression by the independence of the mood periodicity from outward circumstances.
He also found that, unlike hysteria, the cycle of this disease
was impossible to interrupt with hypnosis.

In 1936, the illness was classified by Ernst Kretschmer
as a variation of the cycloid personality temperament. He
made so little of the illness that it was quickly absorbed
into the realm of the normal personality, completely over-
shadowed by the interest in the schizoid, or split personality, and in hysteria. While Vienna and Zurich dominated
psychological awareness, the psychopathology of America

became a national pastime. I want to resurrect the illness of cyclothymia because I think it has something to do with the desire for beauty, a desire to experience the soul of the world.

To begin, listen to some of the metaphors through which Kretschmer describes cyclothymia:

> People of this kind have a *soft* temperament, which can swing to great extremes. The path over which it swings is a wide one, namely between *cheerfulness* and *unhappiness.* . . . There is, however, another swinging path which is very little used, namely that which leads in the direction of *nervous excitability.* . . .
>
> *The cyclothymic is a person of quick temper,* a knightly *hotbloodedness* . . . who *flares* up all of a sudden, and is soon good again. They cannot halt behind a mountain; when anything gets in their way, they see *red* at once, and they try to get what they want by making a row.

Cyclothymia is an illness of the blood, as the word itself tells us — *cyclo-thymia,* the cycling of thymos. *Thymos* is the blood soul — body and psychic vitality united. In the Greek world, thymos was the generator of motion or agitation, that which roused a man to action, and was customarily the abode of joy, pleasure, love, sympathy, and anger. Greek writing sometimes referred to thymos as the raging and boiling of the blood. Said to be in the lungs as the vapor of the liquid of the blood, thymos is a commingling of blood as vitality and breath as psyche. Thymos is active and throbs, beats, quivers, pants, and moves rhythmically. Many commonplace expressions show the quality of thymos — to pant with eagerness, gasp with astonishment, snort with indignation, sob with grief, sigh with sadness.

Blood soul cannot be seen by the hematologist. Like psyche or soul, thymos is not a substance, but neither is it a viewpoint towards things. It carries less the sense of reflection and mirroring, less the imagining of soul, and more the sense of enactment. Thymos as enactment brings soul into action; it concerns the action of the soul of the world in relation to the individual soul. Thymos impels a way of acting in the world rather than a way of reflecting the world; acting with beauty in relation to the soul of the world which reveals itself as beautiful.

Cyclothymia is then an illness of the rhythm of feelings, which need beauty in order to act. What is the matter in cyclothymia is the absence of beauty, resulting in the mood cycles of depression, a turning inward toward individual soul, and nervous excitability, a turning outward to act in soul seeking soul, but finding none. While it has been normalized so that no one is any longer diagnosed with this illness, it nevertheless constitutes a deep malaise of our culture. Nearly daily now, there are newspaper reports of unexplainable violence — quiet, reflective young men suddenly turning to mass murder, like the nice man next door who has twenty bodies stashed in his cellar. In the broad cultural sphere the situation is similar — the cyclothymia of the stock market, cycles of terrorism followed by quiet as if it did not exist, all the swinging of mood and the inescapable nearness of violence. When the soul of the world is diminished, the soul of the individual does not know how to act, it does not experience a setting for its action, and thus explodes all at once.

Since cyclothymia concerns the inability of soul to act because it faces a world seemingly devoid of soul, it might be of benefit to consider the character of soul action, the dramatic character of soul; this in turn may help us recover the action of soul in the world. Jung made an excursion into drama when he once compared the structure of dreams to the structure of dramatic action. He laid out the stages of dramatic structure — statement of place, dramatis personae, exposition, development of plot, culmination or crisis, solution or lysis — and saw dreams as imitating this structure. Since in fact dreams seldom if ever follow such a structure, what was Jung getting at? He was led to the drama of dream by virtue of the fact that the persons and events of dreams are most often partly presentations of persons and events from waking life, what would be called "real," and yet partly imaginal figures — the characters of dreams act unlike they act and present themselves in waking life. So dream characters, the individual presentations of soul in dreams, are like stage actors who are simultaneously real people and imaginal figures. The essence of dramatic figures is such that there is no way to get behind their manifestations. We understand them through their action, through the agony of their tension and movement in relation with each other. Now, if that ambiguity is characteristic of the presentations of the individual soul, so also does it characterize the presentations of the soul of the world; what is real is also image, and the real and the imaginal are inseparable. When the imaginal aspect of the world can no longer be recognized, when the soul of the world becomes repressed so that everything is taken as literal, that is, as being without soul, then the individual soul erupts violently into a world unable to meet its force with counterforce.

Now we get just a little closer to the suffering of cyclothymia by pointing to the agony included in those moments of being torn apart and tearing others apart. What is it that occurs in this agony, so quickly covered over with "good-heartedness," so easily rationalized as just another family argument, a misunderstanding between a man and wife, a bad day at the office, but yet leading perhaps to violence? The temper flare-up of the cyclothymic may be more like a cosmic flare-up than a simple temper tantrum. I want to suggest that the cyclothymic wants to act with soul in a world with soul, but is prevented from acting by a gap that is filled in either of two ways: violence is one way, and now I want to introduce another, addictions. In order to see more clearly the seething cauldron of violence brewing in the world, it is first necessary to see through addiction.

The individual in present society — passive, lost, condemned to a state of consumerism — nevertheless feels that there is something within him that can become a creating force in the world. Such a feeling can initiate a transformative process, a movement into soul, a perceiving of the world as soul. However, this feeling requires two additional phases: initiatory death, and initiatory rebirth. Society allows the first phase, an inner dying, because it is essentially private. But society does not allow the first phase to lead to the second, to the initiatory rebirth. When symbolic death is to lead to rebirth, it entails, for a time, a placing of the present world into doubt, the rejection of one's present view of everything, and the withdrawal of desire from its habitual direction of seeking satisfaction in materialism. The structures of collective life mitigate against such a suspension of belief. For example, a person often spends as much time studying for a profession as practicing it; thus, radical changes of activity are discouraged. Economic structure similarly blocks change — the need to build one's credit by assuming debt fosters a stasis in one's mode of living. Change in the material conditions of life are discouraged. Thus, change in perception of the world comes about only in perverted form, in the form of addictions. In our addictions lie the expectation of the appearance of a magical world. One gives oneself over to a substance that comes from afar and is supposed to carry one far away. The exotic drug is a metaphor for wisdom and psychic/spiritual experience, a metaphor indicating the longing for soul. The process of addiction involves three components, only two of which are presently recognized. First, a physical, organic habit is formed. Then there develops a more subtle habit that forms itself into a kind of conditioning. Finally, the silent, unrecognized component is a striving, an unfruitful quest for an experience of soul and of finding soul in the world. Drug addiction, however, points to a much larger field of addictions to virtually anything — substances, others, position, knowledge, pleasure, money, power, possessions, sex, recognition. Addictions indicate a taking in of the materialistic world view, as if possessing the world would produce completeness of soul. As a symptom of the age, however, addictions indicate that the task of the age is to develop the capacities to experience the world through soul, to actually find soul there in the world. A "new" psychology has formed around addictions; there are twelve-step groups for every addiction imaginable, all based not on the premise that something is missing in the way we face the world, but on remembering an early childhood trauma, raging at the parents or whoever brought the abuse, and then entering a process of recovery that is oriented toward giving oneself over to a higher power, one's self-selected version of an abstraction unrelated to the world. What goes unrecognized in this new psychology is that the "cure" consists of the formation of a new addiction, one perhaps with which living is more comfortable; but since the focus remains on oneself rather than the world, all of life becomes oriented toward the importance of attaining the feeling of self.

When the addiction illusion, which includes the cure, can be put aside, then perhaps it is possible to return to the stage of the world as the setting for the drama of soul. When individual soul encounters world soul, the result is violent, the violence of creative alteration of form. Cyclothymia is but one side of this process, and thus ineffective. In earlier times there existed an imagination of the world undergoing transformation, and this was always pictured as agony, violence, disruption. For example, in *On the EI at Delph*, Plutarch says:

> We hear from the mythographers that the god is by nature indestructible and eternal, but yet under the impulsion of some predestined plan and purpose, he undergoes transformations in his being. . . . When the god is changed and distributed into winds, water, earth, stars, planets, and animals, they describe this experience and transformation allegorically by the terms rending and dismemberment.

The heart of the dramatic imagination of the world is this violent reforming of the cosmos, and when it is possible to really feel the soul of the world, meeting it with soul, a restructuring of soul results. There is no better description for this restructuring than violence, though now we mean not literally enacted violence. When set in motion in the world, imagination diffuses and disperses into unknown, unsuspected forms. Imagination, meeting the world, explodes into a thousand pieces, taking a course beyond dictation. When soul is likewise present in the world, imagination met by imagination, a reconfiguring of the soul of the world comes about with the world as the dramatic space of the soul.

We can look to myths and stories of creation and of recreation to begin feeling the longing for beauty in the imagination of violence. First, a creation myth: In Orphic mythology, Aither is the first born — and there is no limit to it, no bottom or foundation. All things are confusion throughout the misty darkness of Aither. A great silvery egg, a point within Aither, moves in a wondrous circle. From the egg bursts forth Eros — "Female-Father" — described thus: "With four eyes looking this way and that, with four wings moving this way and that, with bulls heads growing on his sides, and on his head a monstrous serpent, appearing in all manner of forms of beasts, a voice of a bull and a lion." Eros built for the immortals an imperishable house — the heavens, the boundless earth, the sea, the constellations, the lowest depths beneath the earth. These things he did through the daughter he bore, Night; when she was born Eros disappeared into Night to work through her darkness. Creation is a violent affair, carried out by a most violent imaginal being in intimacy with the female soul of the world.

In Christian mythology, similarly, the actual creating activities of the material world are carried out by angels. Now, we are used to images of angels as beautiful, winged, long golden-haired humanlike beings. The creating powers of the physical world in this cosmology are the Thrones, one of the angelic hierarchies. In Ezekiel, the Thrones are pictured as many-colored wheel-like structures. These beings are built up in such a way as to form wheels within wheels, multi-colored transparent rings, one turning within the other, the inner one with eyes, and they rise. In recent times the appearance of such beings have been identified as UFO's, and in fact one popular book has taken the account of Ezekiel and said that what he actually saw was a flying saucer. I prefer to work the other way and say that modern accounts of saucers are the appearance of angels; and we see that they work violently. Their appearance is accompanied by a number of disturbing events, electromagnetic interference, witnesses being burned, feeling intense heat or numbness, temporary blindness. The creation of the world, it seems, requires an imagination of violence.

The imagination of a recreation or reforming of the world is the subject of the Greek drama *The Bacchae* of Euripides. This drama begins with the unexpected and untimely appearance of Dionysus within a community devoid of vitality, a community existing only through rigid order, a community epitomized through the figure of Pentheus. Dionysus comes as the violent refiguring of this community, a refiguring that takes place through his confrontation with Pentheus who is dismembered by the maenads. Pentheus is a sacrificial victim. During the encounter between Dionysus and Pentheus, shortly before Pentheus is murdered, Pentheus dons the garb of a woman, imitating Dionysus. That is to say, he is for a moment clothed with the soul of the world, and at that moment his perception of the world changes; he sees double:

> Pentheus: I seem to see two suns, two Thebes, with two times seven gates. And you, you are a bull walking before me, with two horns sprouting from your head.
>
> Dionysus: You see what you ought to see.

This doubling — Pentheus seeing two things at the same time — is like experiencing the depth of imaginal reality while at the same time trying to experience the world in the same old way. There is the sun seen through the depth of imagination, and then there is the "real" sun; the two never quite cohere for Pentheus. He is like the cyclothymic; the temper and rage of the cyclothymic prefigure his own impending dismemberment: they suggest the possibility of a restructuring, but they are met by a rigid world order. In *The Bacchae*, the death of Pentheus does not result in a renewal of the community. For reforming, soul must be recognized in both places at once — in here and out there. When violence erupts without provocation, as part of the mood swing from soul to world without soul, we are witnessing ineffectual sacrifice. During the fifth century, at the same time Euripides was writing, Empedocles was recognizing the prevalence of ineffectual sacrifice. His Fragment 137 says:

> The father seizes hold of the son, who has changed form; in his mad delusion he kills him, murmuring prayers. The son cries out, imploring his insane executioner to spare him. But the father hears him not, and cuts his throat, and spreads a great feast in his palace. In the same way the son takes hold of the father, the children their mother, one slaughtering the other and devouring their own flesh and blood.

Such is the family life of American culture's cyclothymic, filled with bad sacrifice, blood spilt without renewal of soul. The ritual may not involve actual blood; psychic blood, the rending of bonds, of community, and most of all of the bond between individual and world soul makes for contemporary slaughter. Is there a way through the mire of badly spilt blood?

Euripides' drama is ineffectual in renewing the soul of the world because it is written from the point of view of Pentheus, of a Penthean society not unlike our own. When imagination is introduced into such a world, it is either totally ignored, looked upon from a spectator perspective with a degree of fascination, or made to appear as if it could be accommodated without a restructuring of the structures.

If we are to take the dramatic action of soul seriously we must take in the Dionysian world, and in *The Bacchae*, we get only the barest glimpse of that world. The beauty in the Dionysian world is not to be found in his sudden appearance, his madness, his suffering, nor even in the vitality he brings; these aspects alone account only for the passion of soul, not the soul of passion. Marcel Detienne has insight into this soul aspect of Dionysus, seeing it however, as the whole of that world:

> Here we glimpse the inmost secret of his power, the power to cause spurts and leaps. Boiling blood and palpitating wine flow together to form a common principle; the "power" of a vital humor that draws from itself and by itself its capacity to liberate its energy, suddenly, with volcanic violence. Murderous frenzy, leaping maenads, effervescent wine, heart drunk with blood, all aspects of a single mode of action.

Dionysus alone seems to bring about renewal through destruction; but there are other stories, the most important of which link Dionysus with Ariadne. On the island of Crete Theseus slew the Minotaur with the help of wise Ariadne. The Minotaur was a monster who lived in the labyrinth; King Minos had constructed the labyrinth. The name Minos comes from *menes*, or mind, that is to say intelligence. Reason built the labyrinth, but it is the thread through the labyrinth given by Ariadne that allows safe passage through the convolutions. This thread is none other than the thread of logic, and the labyrinth a temple representing the convolutions of the brain; without the thread of intelligence, passage through is impossible. The union of Dionysus and Ariadne, then, brings vitality into connection with beauty, the beauty of imaginal thought, labyrinthine thought, rhythmic heart brought into conjunction with female reason. In imagining Ariadne united in the bloodstream with Dionysus, we have intimations of the cure for cyclothymia: a blood-soul marriage, giving depth to action and action to the presence of imaginative thought. As a way of seeing how soul can act in the world of soul, we can now say that for our time what is required is that imagination become a fully conscious way of thinking which is fully connected with the body.

As imaginal figures of the dramatic action of soul in the world, Dionysus and Ariadne must be considered a tandem — their relationship is characterized as the most faithful in all of Greek mythology. In this mythology we find the story of a second Dionysus, not the god of violent disruption, but nonetheless the god of disruption. This Dionysus traveled from Europe to far distant India, crossed over into Arabia, went through Libya, returning again through Egypt, everywhere teaching the arts of agriculture, the cultivation of the vine, science, writing, the arts. Here he teaches the reality of the soul of the world and the conscious restructuring of the world through soul.

Now, to fully feel the import of the Dionysus-Ariadne tandem, it is necessary to feel how imaginative thinking is not a matter of thinking abstractly. This kind of new thinking is central to the life force of the body; it involves understanding working right into the depths of the body, enacted in the movement and rhythm of the blood. This tandem concerns the permeation of the body and of thought with soul, producing the consciousness soul, which has nothing to do with what is dry and abstract. It is only when one feels that the seeking of imaginative knowing is a matter of life itself that this tandem is present. But remember, from the perspective of those who do not experience this permeation of body with soul, the enthusiasm for learning to see the world through soul and the enthusiasm for learning to see the soul in the world, looks like madness.

Having seen more deeply into what is involved in the malady of cyclothymia our image of it changes radically. The cycling of depression and nervous excitability does not prove to be a cycling at all; the pattern insufficiently carried out is more like a labyrinthine path, not a circle. Ariadne, who carries the epithet "mistress of the labyrinth," suggests that the pattern of the consciousness soul is labyrinthine, a meandering, like a thread going through the convolutions of a shell, passing through the dark recesses of things as well as places well lit. This meander pattern found in numerous Greek temples pictures a winding path that turns back on itself. On this path, the path of soul's dramatic action, the familiar is returned to over and over again, always from another point of view and as a result of experience gained. Socrates describes the labyrinth in Plato's dialogue, *Euthydemus:* "Then it seemed like falling; we thought we were at the finish, but our way bent round and we found ourselves as it were back at the beginning, and just as far from that which we were seeking first." This kind of thought-in-action defeats the idea of having an idea, implementing it, and achieving a set goal. The purpose of the consciousness soul seems to be to engage in image consciousness of the world, which is a kind of repetition of the soul's action in the world; the aim is engagement, to go through the process, finding soul in the process because soul is the process. Meditation, contemplation, dream work, and all such moves inward, whether they be downward or upward, are ineffectual. So are all the outward moves of direct action — getting it all out, letting the festering wounds of anger vent, blood-letting the emotions. Contrary to the admonition of all psychiatric and psychological literature that acting out must be prevented, the only cure for cyclothemia is acting out: the acting out of soul. For this, dramatic imagination turns neither exclusively to an inner world with all its magnificent figures, nor exclusively to an outer world engaged in heroic activity to change the face of things. The action of soul with consciousness remains in the miraculously confusing danceground of joy and agony, experiencing the explosion of image into world and world into image.

Thought today has no vitality because it is dead thought. When we think, we are aware of the object of thought, but not aware of the process of thinking itself. We sleep through the thinking and find ourselves facing thoughts that have already been thought. That is to say, we live outside of our own thinking, aware only of the products of thinking, not the action. Because we do not experience the activity of consciousness, we live in the image of our own being as already finished, and similarly approach the world as if it were already finished. In this situation of diseased consciousness, it becomes necessary to continually be told what to do and how to act from the outside —by others, by authority, by institutions, by attachments, by power. This all-pervasive disease of consciousness is difficult to recognize precisely because it is all- pervasive. If the whole world is a hospital for the sufferers of a malady of consciousness, then society will consider as ill and try to cure anyone who does not suffer the disease. If, for example, the whole world says that success is what is healthy, then anyone not working for success is deemed ill. If one, however, sees success from within the labyrinthine path, sees the kind of soul involved in success, sees also what success looks like from the point of view of the soul of the world, well, the whole quality of success changes. One thinks it through thoroughly from the side of the individual and from the side of the world and this thinking through becomes a way of ensouling. This kind of thinking forms the path to freedom because the forces of the soul have been released.

We find this direction of soul movement in individual development. In the early life of a person, during childhood, all the powers of the soul are bound up in bodily development; they make the body. Later, during adolescence, the soul forces go into the development of the ego — the ego is simply consciousness as a mirror of the body. By body here I mean not only the physical structure, but the thoughts, the memories, the sensations, the images that one already has; these are all reflected in what is called the ego. Later these creating forces of soul become more and more free. They are no longer bound to the development of the body or of the ego and become a kind of surplus of creative soul forces. The question becomes — what happens to these soul forces? They can become trapped in egotism, at both an individual and at a cultural level. In earlier ages, these free creative forces of soul were taken up and formed by religions. No one felt these creative soul forces belonged to themselves; they were felt as belonging to the gods. Now we are independent of the gods, and we are free to choose what to do with those creative soul forces. They can be fed into ever increasing egotism, or they can be freely directed toward establishing, in full consciousness, a connection with the soul of the world, enlivening and sustaining soul in both the individual and the world. Depth psychology has been one-sided, seeking to give attention to these soul forces as occurring only within. This tends to foster an imitation religion and the elevation of subjectivity to the status of religious experience. It produces bad art and a form of ritual in which individuals worship themselves thinking that they are honoring some deity within. Because world is left out of the picture, not only does the soul of the world go unrecognized and neglected, but the exclusive concentration within cannot sustain itself without turning into a system of dead thought.

* * *

Violence belongs to imagination as its inherent shaping force, and when it does not have the container of image it goes wild because something essential has been removed. In present culture violence itself has become a dominant image as if it were expressing a need for attention. Nearly every contemporary film centers on violence and lack of beauty. At the same time a new psychological subculture centering on abuse relies on remembering the presence of violence in early life. These two tendencies form a peculiar duality; on the one hand there seems to be an insatiable need for violence, while on the other it is seen to be the most destructive element in human development. One might say that violence in films is just fantasy, while early childhood abuse is real, but such a division lacks subtlety. Violence portrayed on the screen relies on the feeling of real violence and violence recalled from early life relies on the ability to imagine, while both lack the capacity of looking at what may be involved in violence that makes it so compelling.

Violence in the absence of an awareness of image and soul constitutes a transgression. But there is still the possibility that the violence will be fruitful when led to the element of soul. Michel Foucault points to this most important aspect of transgression when he describes violence as profanation in a world that no longer recognizes the presence of a sacred element. He prescribes transgression as the sole manner of discovering the sacred in its unmediated substance, and, he feels that the composition of violence is scintillating because it points toward what is absent. Violence is thus equivalent to longing. In the absence of soul, desire lacks a "whiter" and shows itself only as the sense of incompletion. With this insight we are led to the recognition of the three siblings of violence —jealousy, envy, and hatred. Envy is a transgression against another in which one wants what the other seems to have — soul. Jealousy is a transgression in which one carefully and suspiciously guards what one believes to be one's possession — the soul of another. Hatred is the action of transgressing, the trangression's *modus operandi*. When one searches around the individual psyche for the sources of violence, envy, jealousy, and hatred and for a cure, none can be found. These phenomena are individually incurable because they belong to cultural psychopathology as the climatic conditions signaling loss of soul in the world. The alteration of these conditions requires that soul be free to do the work of imagemaking, with violence as the sharp force within image work, the engraving quality of image, its divine rage.

LETTER IX

Food: A Case History

DEAR FRIEND,

Food is in a very bad situation in our time, and this is due to what could be called its excessive mineralization; that is, a most important realm of the soul of the world has been taken over into the domain of chemicals. I want to consider food, without however making a case for natural, organic, health food because that is like saying that the way through the difficulties presented by the loss of soul is to return to nature. What I have been attempting in these letters is to suggest, not a return to nature but a return to soul, and now we want to explore what that might imply in the realm of food.

We begin by clearing away all mechanistic, quantitative notions of eating and of nutrition such as number of calories, amount of fat, protein, percentage of daily requirements of substance taken in the daily diet. This mechanistic view of diet began in the 1780s with the work of Lavoisier where we find the origin of the doctrine that life is a chemical function and foods are the combustibles. Nutrition was considered a combustion process in which foods were seen as carriers of caloric energy, which, in conjunction with oxygen, released energy in the digestive process. Other factors have since been added, but it is still a matter of counting. Instead, we begin with the question of what happens when we eat, changing the outlook from quantity to action.

Eating is like an invasion of the body from a foreign world; every food is a kind of poison because it is a foreign

substance taken into the body, and the work of the body is
to transform substance into soul. Eating is an alchemical
work. If we are to consider chemical processes at all it is to
be done with a viewpoint toward soul. For example, gas
bubbles in the stomach initiate hunger, but what is significant here is the connection between hunger and pain in the
soul life. Similarly, the act of swallowing is accompanied
by two acts of consciousness. Food in the stomach, of
which there is a vague experience, is like dream consciousness, while food in the small intestine, of which we are
little conscious, is like the realm of sleep. Going through
dream and sleep, food loses completely its outer form and
even must lose its chemical composition to be recreated as
body — body, not physiology. That is to say what begins as
substance goes through actions that result in the formation
of the soul body. This transformation occurs through the
action of digestion, a rhythmic activity. In the process of
digestion the substance disappears, as it were into rhythm,
the rhythm of the body. Gerhard Schmidt has pointed out
that this rhythm of the body takes place in a 4:1 ratio
between the rhythm of circulation and the rhythm of
respiration, a rhythm that recreates the ratio of movement
between the earth and the sun. We do not simply assimilate
the various chemicals inherent in foods; rather, the body
must take foreign substance and transform it into rhythmic
activity in which the soul of the body resonates with the
soul of the world. Thus, eating is a work against nature.
Schmidt says:

> If man takes up something from the outer world, it is
> injurious to his inner organism, and it is essential that
> the body work against it. . . . We really do not eat so we
> get this or that food into us; we eat so that we develop
> those soul forces which work against these foods. We eat
> in order to resist the forces of the earth and we live on
> earth because we exercise resistance.

Eating, then, is a kind of disease, and digestion the
healing. Substances provide the impetus, the activation of

certain soul forces necessary to ensoul the body, forces which then densify into the particularity of the physical body. Eating is much more like a homeopathic process than a mechanistic or chemical process. Take for example, vitamins. Vitamin A occurs in the parts of plants where warmth predominates — fruits and blossoms. Rather than being a chemical substance, vitamin A introduces into the body a kind of disease of warmth that the soul forces of the body must come up against by developing the quality of warmth. Vitamin B occurs in seeds and husks of seeds, like rice. The husk of a seed is its shaping force, what gives the seed its order. A vitamin B deficiency means that the ordering capacity of the body diminishes; muscle fibers dissolve or separate and paralysis or nerve degeneration eventually results. Taking vitamin B brings in this foreign order-forming substance which stimulates the soul to develop its order-forming capacity in resistance against the foreign material. Vitamin C occurs in green leaf foliage. A deficiency of vitamin C results in scurvy, which shows as a yellowing of the skin or a breakdown of the skin. It is as if one has been shut off from light and put into a dark room to live. Vitamin C is like light, and taking in this substance activates soul to produce its own light.

Now, it might seem that modern, chemical nutrition is on the right track, that what we are actually entering into is an age in which soul is packaged, added to foods in the exact right amount, and that modern eating is soul making. However, I do not believe that soul making can occur in the absence of a consciousness that is oriented toward soul. In addition, the chemical and vitamin additives to food counter each other — for every vitamin added you will find alongside the name of some bizarre chemical. Further, the vitamins themselves are now artificially produced and thus are dummy imitations, doubles of what vitamins are all about. I suspect that instead of the body's being given food that ensouls there is an increasing desouling of body that results in the loss of body's subtlety, that results in the making of body that matches the materialism of a world lacking in soul. My suggestion is that rather than seeking the way out by going natural perhaps new soul forces can be activated by giving attention to the soul suffering of food.

* * *

In order to follow through on the suggestion that the task of the age is to make the activities of soul conscious, let us take a case history of food, a soul history of the primary food of earth, bread. The symptoms: Bread suffers from uniformity. This uniformity presents itself first in terms of the neat wrapper. Bread shows forth no individuality, only the conformity of a small number of bread corporations. Neither hand nor eye can detect one package of bread as different from any other package of bread. Second, bread suffers from unsubstantiality. It is light, airy, soft, frothy, porous, elastic. This is due to the combination of yeast fermentation, carbonic acid which is injected to increase the fluff, high speed mixing rather than kneading, and a high percentage of sugar which makes for looseness of structure; in addition, this lack of substance comes from the injection of chemicals to reinforce the keeping qualities of bread. This suffering of bread extends to rye and whole-wheat varieties as well. Nearly half of the flour of these breads is bleached with gas and mixed with the rye and wheat.

As Freud was led deeper into the defensive outer covering of the crusty ego deeper into the psyche, by paying attention to phenomena such as slips of the tongue, we may develop a similar practice of breaking through the thin crust of bread neurosis by paying attention to the slips of the tongue in our bread language. When we go to the store, we still say that we are purchasing a "loaf" of bread — an obvious slip of the tongue since the uniformity of bread requires that it be a *package* not a loaf. This slip of the tongue is worthy of analysis. The latin word *gleba* is a word expressing the sensation of the earth; the moist, fat loam of the cultivated field was described with the consonant *glb*.

Gleba gives rise to the word *globe,* which signifies not any sphere, but the sphere of cultivated earth. The word *hlaf* which gives rise to *loaf* is etymologically related to *glb,* occurring as a consonantal shift. In other words, *globe* and *loaf* are essentially the same words. The word *bread* is relatively late in origin; it does not appear before the eleventh century, and refers to something that has been brewed. A loaf of bread is thus a sphere of cultivated earth that has been brewed.

While our outer desires now seek what is sweet, smooth, unsubstantial, outwardly appealing, there exists in the language of the psyche a connection with the cultivated earth in ferment. That is, bread is a primary instance of nature taken over into a new sphere of nature put through an alchemical process and cultivated into soul; that is the essence of bread.

I take a second image concerning the soul of bread from an early 1900s novel by Frank Norris, *The Octopus.* Frank Norris was interested in writing an epic, an epic as important as Moby Dick. Nothing, it would seem, could match the elemental cunning and awe which Melville found called forth in man against the whale, an embodiment of the hostility to man latent in unspoiled nature. Whereas Melville pits civilization against nature, Norris pits the corporation against wheat. When he was twenty-nine, Norris wrote the following to a friend:

> I have an idea of a series of novels buzzing in my head these days . . . my idea is to write three novels around the subject of wheat. First, a story of California (the producer), second a story of Chicago (the distributor), third a story of Europe (the consumer), and in each to keep the idea of this huge niagara of wheat rolling from West to East. I think a big epic trilogy could be made out of such a subject that would be at the same time modern and distinctly American. The idea is so big that it frightens me at times, but I have about made up my mind to try it.

In the first chapter of the book, S. Behrman, a company man in what these days would be called agribusiness, agriculture taken over into the realm of the machine, is inspecting a ship in port which is to take wheat to Asia. He stumbles and falls into the hold of the ship, into which the grain elevator is spewing wheat:

> The steady, metallic roar of the pouring wheat drowned out his voice. He could scarcely hear himself above the rush of the cataract. Besides this, he found it impossible to stay under the hatch. The flying grains of wheat, spattering as they fell, stung his face like wind-driven particles of ice. It was a veritable torture; his hands smarted with it. Once he was all but blinded. Furthermore, the succeeding waves of wheat, rolling from the mound under the chute, beat him back, swirling and dashing against his legs and knees, mounting swiftly higher, carrying him off his feet.

Here, wheat shows herself in struggle with the forces of the mechanical reaper and the corporate system, flowing, spreading, engulfing, a dreadful substance that is neither solid nor fluid, creeping, crawling, rushing, dark and suffocating.

Norris was on to something, but it would never succeed like Melville, and we must ask why? This story pictures the soul of the world fighting the hardening forces of mechanization. And she does so by pouring forth her abundance. There are myths of this sort; for example, the story of the Roman general Crassus, whose crass desire for gold brought his death when he was captured by the Parthians who poured molten gold down his throat to sate his greed. Then there is Ovid's story of Erichsicthon who felled a forest of trees and was then visited in a dream by a witch who brought an insatiable hunger which made Erichsicthon devour everything in the land until nothing was left to eat but his own flesh, which he proceeded to do.

Norris' novel, I suspect, was not a success because it

was too subtle, a study of death brought in the form of superabundance. Who could believe in the image of wheat acting as if it were a living being, bringing full force to the mechanized world what has been excluded, the presence of death as belonging to the soul of food? We think that food brings life and have oriented all of the qualities of food toward this image of food as necessary for life. But our look at nutrition has shown quite the opposite. Food is a necessary disease of the body, a poisoning of the body which the soul must counter; it is soul that makes life, needing food to do so. It is the necessary death that food brings that enlivens the action of soul. When food itself is already dead, it is deprived of the capacity to bring death. The reaper is removed from its place in the cosmos as belonging to the grain and becomes the mechanical reaper.

Cyrus McCormick invented the mechanical reaper in the mid 1820s. His father Robert had worked fifteen years without success on the making of such a device. Robert was unsuccessful because he thought of the reaper as a kind of robot, a mechanical man. Cyrus, an engineer, thought solely in terms of machines, machines that would solve an economic problem. The mechanical reaper removed the image of death as belonging to grain and put death into the hands of the engineer. Now, the reaper was not uniquely invented by McCormick. At the same time as his work, a man named Obed Hussey had constructed a similar device. A lawsuit followed in which Hussey sued McCormick. Hussey was supposed to be represented by Abraham Lincoln, but instead was represented by Edwin M. Stanton, who later became secretary of war. On one hot summer day Hussey was sitting on a train in Baltimore; he heard a little girl crying for water. The child was a pretty, golden-haired girl. Hussey got off the train and brought the girl a glass of water. On the way to return the glass, he stumbled and fell underneath the moving wheels of the train; a decisive incident in life that is not unlike the Frank Norris novel, if we can appreciate the image. But mechanization was to

take command, and McCormick won out because we are
dealing here not just with the efforts of some mechanical
geniuses, but a total reconfiguring of the world.

At the same time that McCormick and Hussey were
inventing the reaper, a young German, Leibig, had given up
chemical experiments and moved to the country to set up a
laboratory of the soil. Liebig proved in 1840 that plants
required four chief inorganic chemicals — nitrogen, potas-
sium, lime, and phosphoric acid. Wherever grain was to
grow, these four substances must be present in the soil.
This dioscovery led to the invention of chemical fertilizers.
It would no longer be necessary to rotate crops. Year in,
year out, the same plants could be grown in the same field.
Humus was removed from the sphere of cultivated earth;
that is to say, at the same time that harvesting was
mechanized, its soul removed, soul was also removed from
grain. Humus is earth that has passed through the intestines of worms, earth eaten and excreted, the death that
brings food to life, which in turn must produce the death
which is countered by soul to make the ensouled body.

The underworld component of bread has been removed
and forgotten through the spirit of machinery and the
invention of chemical fertilizer. Thus, harvesting has lost
its connections with death, as has growth. The soul of bread
which remembers and contains the mysteries of the dark
earth has become subservient to a more spiritual fantasy of
quick energy, purity. This transformation of bread was
prepared for in the beginning of Christianity. A radical
change in the imagination of bread occurs at the Last
Supper. Jesus is the new bread god, replacing the mysteries
of Eleusis. Jesus was born in Bethlehem, which means
"house of bread." The parable teachings of Jesus are concerned with the subtle processes of plowing, sowing, harvesting, and bread. He instantly multiplied seven loaves to
feed four thousand. He declared, "I am the bread of life; he
that cometh to me shall never hunger; and he that be-
lieveth in me shall never thirst." And as St. Matthew tells
us: "And as they were eating, Jesus took bread, and blessed

it, and broke it, and gave it to the disciples, and said, 'Take, eat; this is my body.'"

These actions of Christ might seem to have little to do with a package of bread. But we must try to feel how deeply the new god of bread altered the imagination of food. A decisive event in the history of humanity introduced a savior complex into food. Food, because it is now unconsciously connected with the image of Christ as the everlasting bread of life, is connected with the fantasy of everlasting life. Food is no longer connected with rotting or spoiling or decaying or putrefying or stinking, but only with the energy of life. The language of life is calories, proteins, carbohydrates, vitamins. Food itself does not rot or die but is filled with preservatives; it has gone through the rites of purification which ensure its immortality. The optimists of food now feel that it is possible to feed the whole world, to banish hunger from the face of the earth, and to do so by disrupting the traditions of agriculture, replacing them with mechanisms and chemicals.

Now, to be precise, it is not Christ who brings about this change, but the interpreters of the highly mysterious events of the life of this individuality. The words of Christ — "This is my body" — for a long time were words inspiring interpretive controversy. The question concerns whether Christ performed a symbolic act or whether he taught that the bread they ate was really his body. The imagination of Christianity lived for a thousand years without having to answer this question decisively. The issue was settled in 1204 by the Lateran Edict. On one side of the argument were the Church Fathers who argued that the actions of Christ were symbolic; this interpretation was based on the gospel of Luke, which adds the words, "Do this in remembrance of me." The other gospels do not contain these words, and thus give rise to the argument, on the other side, that the act is not one of commemoration, but that bread becomes Christ each time these words are said by the priest. The latter argument, that of the realists, won, which is to say Christianity lost its imagination, was no longer able to comprehend the reality of image. A decision in the other direction would have been equally fatal for imagination, for then, the event of Christ's words would be seen as having nothing to do with ongoing reality. The debate that needed to take place but never did concerns the reality of imagination, how image can be real and have real effects in the world. The mentality of the time was incapable of focusing on such a subtle issue and instead split the matter of imagination into two impossible parts: either what Christ said is real and bread does turn into Christ, or what he said is symbolic, the putting forth of a rite of memory that has no direct effect in the actual world. That the issue was resolved in the direction of the realists, I suggest, led to the spiritualization of food. A source of abundance for the soul is bypassed and Christianity instead takes the direction of eliminating soul from the world. We see the making of this savior complex early on in the history of Christianity. Papias, an early Church Father, writing in about 140 A.D., said:

> The days will come in which vines shall spring up, each bearing ten thousand stocks, and on each stock ten thousand branches, and on each branch ten thousand shoots, and on each shoot ten thousand bunches, and on each bunch ten thousand grapes, and each grape when pressed shall yield five and twenty measures of wine. Likewise, also a grain of corn shall cause to spring up ten thousand ears of corn, and each ear shall hold ten thousand grains, and each grain ten pounds of fine, pure flour. And so it shall be with the rest of the fruits and seeds and every herb after its kind. And all animals which shall use those foods that are not got from the ground shall live in peace and accord, in all things subject to man.

Today, such a speech could well be made by a secretary of agriculture. The world is said to be moving toward an age of limitless abundance, cybernated food production under the control of computers, remote control cultivators, television monitors, data banks that automatically run thousands of acres of cultivated land, two computer operators feeding millions of people. What is lost in this rhetoric is the fact that such an approach to food production not only produces food without soul, it uses up the land because it makes food without providing for the component of death which is necessary for the renewal of the land. This approach to food derives from the imagery of food infected with spirit — inflated, manic, full of blind hope, concerned with quantity.

Since the time of the interpreters of Christ the imagination of food has more and more involved a detachment from the earth; thus, food is removed from the world, becoming an abstraction. For example, table manners are put forth that have the intention of removing contact from food. Antoine de Courtin, in 1672, wrote a book of manners in which he declared that it is impolite to touch anything greasy, a sauce or syrup, with the fingers. If one touches food then one has to wipe frequently and soil one's napkin; and those who see one wiping will feel nauseated. And, if one does not wipe on a napkin, then one might be compelled to do so on one's bread, or even worse, to lick one's fingers. The fork is to the plate of food as the mechanical reaper is to the field of grain.

Once the earth is detached from food, earth becomes evil. During the plague of 1300 in which gnawing and crawling rats were seen as the carriers of disease, the people thought that the plague came out of the earth itself; they thought the earth was poisoned, that it breathed forth a misty poison. It is more likely that the plague was the result of the removal of connection with the earth. Once having lost continual connection with earth, being at home with rot and decay and knowing that fermentation also belongs to the imagination of the body, the body purified is resubjected to its own discarded infections.

Now to lean in the direction of returning food to earth seems very congenial to natural, organic, health food advocates. The tactic taken against modern food is to show that the chemicalizing of food is dangerous to our health. But natural foods, too, are toxic. An ounce of salt a day can shorten life by thirty years. Nutmeg and avocados can be fatal; onions can cause anemia; spinach and rhubarb cause kidney stones; cabbage causes goiters. The question of removing food from earth, I believe, does not have to do with health, but with care of the soul. The chemical spiritualization of foods, which makes foods available without regard to seasons, which enables foods to last without decay, does something to the imagination of food; it hides the element of death that is necessary to psychic life. The loss of this psychic element can be found in connection with all advances in food production.

In 1850, Gail Borden found that if he added sugar —which in quantity inhibits bacterial growth — to milk, the result was milk that kept well. In the 1840s, a new method of milling flour was introduced in Hungary; iron rollers were used rather than stone mills. The old stone milling pulverized the embryo, or germ, of the grain. It was the oil from the germ that gave flour its characteristic yellow color and also turned it rancid in a few weeks. The new iron rollers squeezed the grain in such a way that the endosperm popped out of its coating, leaving the germ behind to be sieved off with the bran. During the nineteenth century, rice was polished to remove the drab outer shell, and thus the germ of rice was removed. Wherever we see progress in the production of food we find the psychic element of death, the essential element of the soul of the world, removed and discarded.

The change in agriculture and in the production of food has disturbed the relation between the larger macrocosm and the human as a microcosm; that is to say, we have become emancipated from the larger cosmos. There are two ways to view this freedom. One is to attempt to return, which would mean the diminishing of consciousness. The other way is to utilize this freedom to find a way back to relationship through the development of the consciousness soul — to do the work of looking at everything psychologi-cally, through soul. The illusion of emancipation from the larger world, that we are removed from the soul of the world, is sustained through the concept of energy, and energy is central to the modern understanding of food and nutrition. No one today would say that food is for the soul; it is to provide energy to the body. So we must confront this energy fantasy of food.

What is energy? According to contemporary physics, energy is the capacity for activity. Energy is always associ-ated with some process, or some activity. Energy can change form, but none of it can get lost. Relativity theory says that mass is nothing but a form of energy. Mass is no longer associated with material substance, but is now understood as bundles of energy. Matter and activity are no longer separated. Physics builds an elaborate field of knowl-edge on this unknown, immaterial abstract. The term *energy* is spirit filled — activity, spiritedness, vigor, life, power, action, capacity, vitality — all are synonymous with energy. Until we can enter into a more interior sense of the word energy we will remain stuck with food that is ori-ented toward producing energy, not soul.

One way of appreciating the connection between energy and experience is suggested by Alfred North Whitehead in his statement that " the energetic activity in physics is the emotional intensity entertained in life." Emotion, he sug-gests is nothing else than the soul experience of energy. To look upon food, then, as nothing more than a source of energy, to increasingly supply this energy directly, is to remove emotional intensity from the face of the world and package it in the form of energetic food, bypassing the soul in order to keep activity moving.

In the realm of the old psychology, subjective psychol-ogy, there are two corollaries to the view of emotion as energy. The first is that energy is emotion which must be let out, discharged or released. Intensity of emotion is subjectively felt as "heat" of feeling. This view of emotions is like the old view of physics that says material substances contain energy which can be released by applying pressure. There are "therapeutic" techniques which operate in the same manner. Such techniques are called anxiety-provoking therapy, and are oriented toward liberating energy and directing it into socially useful channels. Our view of energy in the world is currently based on exactly this kind of model. The mechanization of food and the view of nutrition as supplying energy follows this kind of model —extract the energy from living food, learn how to make these energetic substances artificially, and eating consists of putting in energy to get energy out. Discharge is seen as inherently good.

A second corollary to the view of emotion as energy is that emotion can be converted or transformed. This is subjective psychology's version of the law of conservation of energy. In psychological theories based upon this view of emotion, when emotion is not converted into energy it causes psychosomatic illness. Energy that is retained in the body as emotion causes body symptoms. Again, the implication is that the job is to direct the flow of emotions into appropriate energy channels before it causes permanent structural damage in the organs.

The notion of matter in the realm of physics and in subjective psychology is that matter is dead, but that if matter is squeezed hard enough you can get life out of it. If emotion, then, is the way that energy appears to consciousness, the energy that comes from matter treated in this way can be named as an emotion, and that emotion is anxiety. That is to say, when food is approached as a source of energy it is approached as a singular emotion, and that emotion is anxiety. We are currently fed on anxiety. The direction nutrition takes when food is reduced to energy, when the emotional intensity of life is reduced to anxiety, can be seen when we look at the direction matter takes when seen as energy — can be seen, that is, in the realm of nuclear energy. Nuclear energy, it seems, cannot be contained, it is as if it has no interior. The present means of containment are all highly defensive — thick concrete, lead, and the ever-present sense of high anxiety. When we put food into the imagination of energy, we are all transformed into nuclear reactors and we require the formation of rigid societal defenses aimed at containing our formless activity.

The analogy between lead-contained nuclear energy and food imagined as energy suggests that the soul may well be on the way to rigidifying. Lead, which can contain nuclear power, results from the disintegration of uranium; that is, frenetic energetic activity lies but a step away from pure inertia. Thus, when the value of food is put into energy the soul body may be inclining toward leadenness. Matter, as pure radiation — matter which has no interior — results in matter that has no radiation at all; the balance between exterior and interior becomes disturbed, divided into an absolute polarity. A further analogy now comes to light. Current new age spiritual practices also employ the metaphor of energy as a central concept — moving energy, balancing it, sending it, receiving it. In all these practices energy is identified with spirit. And the body in such practices becomes more or less disdained. One seeks out-of-body experience, a purification of the body into light; one sees the materiality of body as a limitation to spiritual experience. In such practices the body becomes as if lead —inert and uninvolved in the world. Thus an alliance seems to take place between the materialistic concepts that govern the way food is now imagined and the current imagination of spirit. The two, on the surface, appear to be antagonistic, for often the same people who follow new age practices walk around with bottles of pure spring water, are inclined toward organic health foods, and generally mistrust the world, seeing it as polluted. Materialism, however, consists of more than the single form of a concentration on physical matter; it can equally take the form of a concentration against matter. Both stances exclude the middle ground of the soul. In the case of food, soul on the side of the world is diminished, while in the case of many new age practices, soul on the side of the individual is similarly diminished. The question then arises: how do we stay in connection with soul?

Each of these letters attempts a response to this question, and the direction of each response concerns the work of keeping imagination active, in open connection with fully awake consciousness, and fully related to the world. Now, it hardly seems that such a response, if carried out, would produce any real effects in the world. But the importance of such work lies in feeling the value of something done gradually, with consistency, even when visible effects do not appear forthcoming. In the domain of soul, one cannot make things happen through control. For example, when a relationship between individuals (a prime instance of a realm of soul) goes wrong these days, three directions of action are possible: the couple try to make it work, but only succeed in putting more focus on what is wrong, strengthening the defects by trying to work against them; the couple sever their relationship, and go through the strange procedure of selecting a day and moving out —strange because while it takes years to form a relationship, we are under the illusion that ending it happens all at once; the couple become resigned that nothing can be done and that individually they can only shut down completely and "live" in the situation. Our relationship with the world, when it hurts sufficiently for us to want to do something, follows this same pattern — trying to change the way we live with it, turning away from it, or living with hopeless resignation and bitterness. A fourth alternative would not have us attempt to produce change, turn away, or become resigned, but instead would have us find value in a new act of attention, an act of attention to soul in the midst of the world as it is. Here the effects are immediate because they are one with the cause; the whole world as soul opens for new learning.

LETTER X

World Soul and
Hermetic Consciousness

DEAR FRIEND,

These letters began with a presentation of Sophia as
archetypal figure of the world soul along with an indication
that world-engaged imagination relies on the presence of an
additional form of archetypal image stimulating the capacity to navigate in the world with soul. If the world structures developed in the previous letters were seen only
through Sophia there would be no way or method for
continually interrelating world and soul. At best it would
be possible to enlarge the taken-for-granted sense of the
everyday world by seeking its archetypal background in
soul, a procedure commonly employed in archetypal psychology. But, to keep world and soul constantly together
requires a relating factor, a form of consciousness in service
to the soul of the world which can be named as a particular
mythical presence. The tradition names this figure Hermes
and the kind of consciousness projected by this figure
hermetic consciousness. The concern of this final letter
consists of showing that the preceding letters belong to the
hermetic tradition and that this tradition provides a way for
navigating in the instability of a constantly mobile world of
living image. To introduce hermeticism at the outset of
these letters would hardly have been a hermetic procedure,
and I did not do so for fear that the approach could too
easily be dismissed as occult, or, equally damaging, that the
association could be taken as a formula when the whole

impulse of this mode of consciousness is to dissolve formulations.

The roots of hermeticism go at least as deep as ancient Egypt where it was a highly developed mode of knowing, analogical knowing, knowing through similars. Our most common way of knowing derives not from similars but from opposites, knowing through a division between the knower and the known. Analogy proceeds through a conscious incorporation of the knowing into the known and of the known into the knower, resulting in "living thinking" or mythical thinking. Verification of this way of knowing depends not on accumulation of facts, but on whether or not the subject of interest comes alive, whether it enlivens the knower. Analogy is not intended to replace other modes of knowing, but to suggest that for our time, a time of excessive fragmentation, a much needed synthetic mode of thought in which inner and outer are intertwined can be beneficial. Hermetic consciousness is an image consciousness of the world in which the world presents itself as living image. In this mode, consciousness is not all on our side; but rather, this mode of knowing consists of a continual exchange of consciousness producing a synthesis of soul. The element making possible this ongoing synthesis of soul, I suggest, relates to the archetypal action of Hermes.

The primary document of the hermetic tradition is the Egyptian fragment known as The Emerald Tablet. All alchemy can be traced to this source. In addition, alchemy, as pointed out in the first letter, centers on the world-creating figure of Sophia. While the word *hermetic* is Greek, hermeticism comes under the sign of the Egyptian god Thoth. The Emerald Tablet is attributed to Hermes Trismegistus, said to be an actual human being, the embodiment of Thoth. If Trismegistus was human, our interest lies in his being a channel of Hermes — the name Trismegistus means "thrice greatest Hermes." Hermes works through this figure to create the philosophy, hermeticism. But underlying this philosophy is Hermes, involved in a continual recreating activity, transforming world into image. The Greeks inherited the hermetic wisdom as the myths of Hermes, and thus we have with this figure both a philosophy of the world soul and stories concerning the action of the ongoing creation of the world soul. That is to say, in order to enter into mythical thinking concerning the soul of the world, both these currents have to be followed, the philosophical and the mythological currents. Then, the further task, one that has already been taken up in the letters, concerns enacting this twofold current in a manner applicable to present cultural circumstances. The mistake would be to separate this tradition from the actual goings on of the everyday world and relegate it to the "occult," leaving it to the initiates.

In Egyptian myth Thoth is imaged as an ibis-headed man. The ibis is a very mysterious bird, characterized by its black and white color and its gesture in sleep — when it puts its head under its wing while sleeping, the ibis forms the image of the heart. When the Egyptians wished to write the word *heart,* they drew an ibis. The constantly mobile realm of thought belongs to the region of the birds. In Egyptian times no one considered thought to be a private affair going on within the head or the brain, but rather as a world event, belonging to the air element; birds then are like momentary condensations of the air element, visible thought in the world. That Thoth is in the image of the ibis and that the ibis has such affinity to the heart indicates that hermeticism consists of a thinking of the heart. By the time of the Greeks, thought had descended, so to speak, closer to the human realm, and the image changes from the bird to the mythical figure of Hermes, said to be the god friendliest to man. Thus, the reorientation needed to see the world through soul concerns the image capacity to think through the heart. The Emerald Tablet was meant as a guide to this mode of thought.

Some of the features of this document include the primacy of thinking in terms of likenesses — "that which is above is like that which is below, and that which is below is like that to which is above, to accomplish the miracle of one thing." Here we see that the perception of likeness requires the imagination of depth. Similarity cannot be seen when one looks only through the senses; one must see through the depth of imagination to perceive soul through soul. Then a second requirement involves the necessity of perceiving the commonality of soul while retaining the particularity of each thing of the world. The Emerald Tablet provides for this as follows: "And as all things were by contemplation of the One, so all things arose from this one thing by a single act of adaptation." As soul makes all things, there is a unique agent which adapts each thing made by soul to its particular use. The question that this statement presents is, what is this unique agent? It is not a what, but a who. I suggest it is Hermes, who in Greek mythology turns out to be threefold.

Greek myth presents images of the multiple creating actions of soul. But it is particularly through Hermes that these image-making actions become world centered and human centered at the same time. The determination of the essence of the Greek gods and goddesses belongs to the art of the poet. Without the poet we are faced with fragmented historical conceptions of gods and goddesses that vary according to local regions and cities. Thanks to the poet the countless local cults of Greece were brought together into a true image, a permanent configuration assembled in one superterrestrial abode, Olympus. Olympus functions as an imaginal place, a "mundus imaginalis," in the words of Henri Corbin. Through this place all actual places and beings come forth. The Homeric Hymns constitute the poetic mythology of the archetypal creating beings of soul and are what the great mythologist Mircea Eliade calls "true stories." Eliade says these stories differ from tales and fables which, even though they cause changes in the world, have not altered the human condition as such. Myths, or true stores, do alter the human condition; something occurred that has altered the fabric of time itself. The Homeric Hymn to Hermes reveals the particular alteration that allows the action of soul in the world. Without Hermes, the realm of soul would involve another world — either Olympus or perhaps the Underworld, but not this, our everyday world.

Hermes is the son of Zeus and a cave nymph, Maia. Maia warrants particular attention. The nymphs are neither human nor divine. They are associated with the very source of life, and thus are found in groves of trees, near fresh springs, new plants, wherever life is emerging. Standing as more or less midway between mortal and immortal, nymphs are the wetnurses of divine children. Maia is such a wetnurse to Hermes, and she is very special. In one place she is named the daughter of the Titan Atlas, and in another place she is said to be the eldest star of the constellation known as the Pleiades. She spans the complete range of being, from the highest to the lowest, and is the bearer of the interchangeability of the highest with the lowest. She is, I believe, one of the faces of Sophia. Hermes serves the full range of these archetypal dimensions, from the lowest bodily function to the highest, most lofty abode of the gods. The alchemists fully understood their patron, Mercurius, for their efforts concerned finding soul in all things, and it is Hermes who is the distributor of soul, servant of Sophia, creating hermetic consciousness.

What is hermetic consciousness? Thievery, trickery, cunning, magic, all that has to do with keeping imagination moving — these are the attributes of Hermes. Such attributes are necessary for the task of enacting soul throughout the things of the world for imagining soul in the world. The Olympian world, when completed — this place outside time — forms a static universe. The hermetic theft brings mythical configurations into world events while never allowing the world events to lose their quality of physical closeness. Through Hermes the immortal becomes intimately linked with the temporal world of mortals. And, in turn, the temporal world of mortals becomes infused with the imagination of the timeless and permanent. Thus, Hermes is the god presiding over the borders, making possible commerce between the divine and the human. Further, this commerce suggests that the soul world is affected, changed by what occurs in the human world, that the realm of soul is affected by how we see things, that the commerce is two-way. Let us consider this theft of Hermes as presented in the Homeric Hymn.

On the day following his birth Hermes leaves the dark seclusion of the cave of his origin and ventures forth into the sunlight. But we must never forget his origin in night, for night is not just a time but a state of consciousness. It is not a state of sleep, for we are also told in many ways of the constant mental agility of Hermes — his restless powers of observation, his glance that swiftly lights on all relevant details and misses nothing of importance, his lightning-swift intelligence that cuts through all obstacles to reach its goal. These two qualities — night consciousness and intelligence — taken together give a real feeling for hermetic consciousness. Hermetic consciousness is like entering into a state of darkness that is nonetheless light, like seeing things in a flash that are invisible to the senses. At the moment Hermes leaves the cave, at that very transition from night to light, he spies a tortoise. Persuasively, seductively, deceptively, he speaks of seeing new possibilities for the tortoise, which he proceeds to kill, and from the shell, he invents the lyre. That is, Hermes sees in a flash the soul element of the tortoise and makes it into a work of craft, a work of art. That is the kind of intelligence I am talking about — not logical, but swift, incredibly creative, sometimes cruel, seeing the soul possibilities in the moment. This kind of image-making intelligence makes possible the enjoyment of living in the world through soul, and without it soul must be suppressed in order to gain a sense of stability.

And there is a type of force associated with this mode of image intelligence. Hermes comes up against Apollo, the god concerned with maintenance of order and hierarchy and separations. Hermes is able even to win Apollo over, an indication that hermetic consciousness can bring about alterations in the world that seems fixed. Not only does Hermes win over Apollo, in so doing he brings about an equality among the gods, for the cattle that Hermes steals from Apollo become a feast celebrating the equality of the gods. This craftily prepared feast looks like a sacrifice to the gods, but it is not. Hermes kills two of the stolen cattle, divides up the meat into twelve portions to honor the pantheon, in which he includes himself. The twelve portions are equally divided. If it were a sacrifice to the gods and goddesses, each god and goddess would be given an unequal share, a portion in proportion to the deity's particular degree of honor. Instead, we have here a feast that brings in a new element, an element that says when, through Hermes, the gods and goddesses are brought into close connection with the mortal world, they are all equal; each has an equal part to play in the realm of becoming, in the soul of the world. In the timeless realm of being, Olympus, the deities all have their separate domains and are hierarchically arranged. In the temporal order of becoming, all are equal; soul is equally distributed. Thus, we have two of the three dimensions of "Thrice Greatest Hermes": he establishes commerce, a continual exchange between the gods and the mortals, bridging the gap that would otherwise exist between the soul world and this world; and he establishes commerce between the gods who otherwise rule over their separate domains, bringing about the equal sense of soul in all matters of the world. But there is a third aspect as well.

When Hermes steals Apollo's cattle, Apollo goes stalking the culprit and takes him before Zeus. Boldly, Hermes denies the accusations of Apollo, but is reconciled with Apollo when he gives him the gift of the lyre that he created from the tortoise. First, Hermes sings, and his song is a theogony, a new theogony establishing commerce of soul throughout the world. He then gives Apollo the lyre, a very clever move which wins him over by giving him an instrument that is at the same time a new way of ordering things, for the lyre brings the possibility of singer and player being the same individual. This gift also images the intimate connection between a soul realm of a god and the soul realm of something of the world and how they must relate — through rhythm. Now, Apollo is delighted and gives Hermes the caduceus. The caduceus is the magical wand carried by Hermes. The modern version of the caduceus is the emblem of the medical profession, which undoubtedly has lost the memory of its origin, and, more tragically, has lost the whole concept of healing with which the instrument is connected. The two intertwining snakes, which at the top of the instrument face each other, signify soul confronting soul in an act of regeneration, the recreative act of commerce between individual and world soul. At the moment Hermes receives this instrument Zeus gives Hermes the exclusive right to penetrate into the Underworld and to carry souls to Hades. This takes us to the third domain of "Thrice Greatest Hermes." He crosses the boundaries of the gods' and goddesses separations from each other; he bridges the boundary between the divine and the human; and he bridges these two realms with the Underworld.

The territory belonging to Hermes is transition across borders, and it is of the utmost importance that we remember that his transits always go both ways. The caduceus has a twofold power. It puts souls to sleep and it awakens them again. Here, then, we are taken into a great mystery. Hermes, as Petronius says later in history, "is the one who leads souls away and leads them back again." Hermes has the power of the regeneration of soul.

The image confirming that indeed the third great gift of Hermes concerns the regeneration of soul is the much misunderstood image of the herm. The word herm means "stone heap," and also refers to a particular phallic image of Hermes placed along the road as a guide for travelers, and also at the borders of particular precincts. The herm is a peculiar image — a stone statue of Hermes that is but a plain block lacking hands and feet, but which exhibits an erect phallus and typically a bearded head of the god. One additional aspect of the herm is of great importance — it rests on a square base. Our question of this image is simply this: how does soul regenerate? The image indicates that soul returns to world through the phallus. However, Hermes is not to be confused with gods associated with sexuality or with love. The intent of this image is not sexual or erotic. Further, and this I know is difficult, but it must be said, this phallic herm is as much feminine as it is masculine; nay, even more strongly put, the essence of this image is feminine insofar as what is depicted here is Hermes emerging from the very source of life, from the four-sided base, from the four soul elements forming the world soul, which in alchemy are the elements of Earth, Air, Fire, and Water. The herm does not so much rest on top of the square base as it emerges from the base, coming up from the Underworld. Once this aspect of the image is seen, the phallus takes on a particular meaning. It may be more clear if I say it very directly: the phallus is merely the conduit through which the seed, or soul, is transported into the world. That the herm also shows the head of Hermes indicates further that the regeneration of soul in the world, while an act of service to Sophia, also requires the clear consciousness of the head, that is, of imaginal thought. Through meditative intelligence, rooted in the world soul, soul regenerates in the world. Thus, the image of the herm carries out in reverse, mirror-image the transitions, the boundary crossings that we have seen in the other direction with the first two aspect of threefold Hermes — as above so below, so say the alchemists.

Hermetic philosophy and Hermes mythology present a picture of modern hermetic consciousness. This consciousness consists of the capacity of seeing through the invisible flow of back and forth connections relating one thing to another, individual to world soul. This mode of image consciousness is not a natural gift, but must be earned through experience, through the discipline of creating connections between opposites, the practice of intuitive intelligence. This practice requires the development of the ability to concentrate without effort. Just as the magician or juggler or wire walker had to train and work for a long time before attaining the ability of concentration without effort, so too, those who make use of intuition have acquired long experience and teaching. At the same time, the work of the hermeticist is always play. The hermeticist makes, through taking or thieving what the world has to offer and twisting it into new forms, a synthesis between creative spontaneity and deliberately executed consciousness.

Let me summarize a few additional aspects of hermeticism as related to the task of facing the world with soul. The work of hermeticism is solitary. Thus, what has been put forth in the letters on the soul of the world can never be put into a "school of thought"; the letters serve only as an invitation, an encouragement to begin facing the world in new ways. The solitary nature of the venture is well illustrated by the Tarot card of the Hermit, who is the hermeticist. The Marseilles deck pictures the Hermit as a solitary individual holding in his right hand a lantern and leaning on a staff. He is dressed in a red robe under a blue mantle. The lantern pictures the light of intuition. That the Hermit stands alone indicates that he has separated himself from collective imagination in order to listen to the soul of the world. This is his mantle — to stand alone, but to stand in and for the soul of the world. He leans on a staff; that is, he is in immediate connection with the ground, and he advances only after having touched the ground of immediate experience. He proceeds by way of intuition, analogy, and experience. That he holds the lamp of intuition suggests that what he knows and what he sees does not come from his own intellect, from his brain, but from a light in the world. What counts as reality is not his individual thoughts but what shows forth in the world through the light of intuition; the lamp unites intellect with things, and thus he proceeds neither through opinion nor personal feeling, but through the light of consciousness in the world. And he stands out in the world with no apparent aim. He is not out to accomplish something for himself, but stands as a servant, feeling his way in the darkness. Further, he is in the process of walking — his way of thinking is mobile, not stationary, it proceeds from quality to quality.

Now, the question arises: once it becomes clear what is involved in the style of work carried out in these letters, who would want to be engaged in such a task? The question must be responded to from a cultural rather than an individual point of view. The cultural world is no longer stable. It is no longer possible to come into life, grow up in a family, work hard, achieve results, rely on the presence of tradition, feel the living sense of history, and feel fully engaged in the immediacy of the world. We now have to create situations out of soul in the face of a seemingly soulless world. We are entering a time of total instability. Absolutely no one will be unaffected by or protected from this worldwide shifting that shall accelerate in the near future. This instability is already visible and apparent. Since this time of crisis concerns the world as a whole, it would seem decidedly ineffective to suggest the development of a solitary style of relating to the world. One looks for some collective gathering, some movement — political, social, or even spiritual — but certainly not to the suggestion that the primary task of the age is to face the world with soul.

Facing the world with soul does require the development of the soul capacity to work toward individual soul experience held in conjunction with world soul — to be solitary, but not isolated. The gnostics had a term for this stance; such people were called the *monachoi*, which means "solitary ones," but which also means "those who have become unified." The monachoi are those who have succeeded in freeing themselves from the dominion of the tyrant of collectivity, and have achieved a true community of the soul. Being solitary and being in a community do not seem to go together; but that is because we suffer from many illusions concerning the nature of community. Community, like the collectivity, can be an imitation, a double, not based on true individuality of soul but on collective common interests that demand that the individual compromise what is in his heart for the benefit of the group. We must look further into the notion of community from the viewpoint of soul.

First, we can say what community is not. It is not the feeling of warm coziness, founded on the model of the family, that produces bondage rather than freedom; it is not calculating — seeking to join forces with others in order to produce collective force; it is not gathering together into groups. In the medieval world, the Grail legend provided an image for the community of soul. The Grail was not something one had, but the mysterious object of a quest; the value of the Grail was in the search for it. *Parzival*, the poem that tells the story of this search, consists of 718 sections, a number that is an image indicating the multiplicity of approaches needed in the forming of the community of soul. Further, the word *Grail* means "gradually" —the value is in something that emerges over time but is never defined. That something is both an outlook toward the world as soul and an outlook toward others as soul. Being in community implies doing things out of full individuality, and it means having the ability to see others as if they belonged to the mysteriousness of my own soul and as if they belonged to the mysteriousness of the soul of the world. It demands that I experience full autonomy of soul, that I live a connection in which my individual soul experience becomes more complete as I more fully perceive and acknowledge the individuality of other souls. Destiny reveals itself slowly and remains hidden when coerced to comply with any model or conception of collective mentality.

It may be a very new concept to consider community as the conscious choice to be concerned for soul, to want the soul experience for others, but to refrain from defining how it should appear. When community does show forth among people it shows in the word, the living, creative, unexpected, heartfelt, spontaneous, thoughtful, reflective speaking through which the soul of the world finds voice. The showing forth of soul does not belong to any group, least of all groups specifically oriented toward making soul happen — it does not come through inner journeys, dream work, multimedia extravaganzas of the image, poets, artists, environmentalists, group work, feminism, masculinism, conferences, Gaia groups, new physics, transpersonal psychology. Attending any such gatherings one quickly discovers that soul finds voice there in no greater frequency than in a group of people gathered to talk about neighborhood crime, or at a board meeting of the local school district, or at the weekly city council meeting. The wisdom of soul is dispersed equally in the world, it seems, and it is likely that it works least in those situations that are organized into money making propositions, that put forth claims that here is where and how soul is to be found.

If facing the world with soul requires hermetic solitariness which nevertheless takes place in a community of soul, but if such a community is never organized or made explicit, where then, does one find the means to develop the discipline to enhance what one already feels or knows in a vague way, where does one find the courage to stick to the inner conviction of the centrality of soul? Well, like the Hermit of the Tarot, one becomes an itinerant traveler — a traveler through the tradition, seeking in books, in the world, in the immediacy of experience, in what is said or done by others, in an active love of the world; and one always learns, always moves, always seeks depth, but never becomes an adherent to any of these sources. The background for this manner of proceeding was prepared in the Florentine Academy where Marsilio Ficino was given the task of translating the ancient documents known as the Hermetica. Today, we take for granted that one can walk into any bookstore and find any tradition whatsoever — Indian, Sufi, Cabala, alchemical, Taoist, and all the rest. This availability of wisdom is so commonplace that we hardly give it attention. But it can all be traced back to that moment when Ficino was interrupted from his work on

Aristotle and told to translate some strange documents. The result of that work is that the traditions of wisdom no longer belong to sects or cults but to the world at large. And they are in the world at large not so that would-be modern initiates might take them up and leave this world to enter into the past; rather, we must take what immediately presents itself — these traditions have entered into the world at large. The new temple of initiation is the world itself.

Now, I am not saying simply that anyone can now do in the comfort and privacy of the home what formerly only certain individuals could accomplish — by going to the places of soul wisdom and there finding a teacher and there going through years of training to enter into the practices that result in spirit and soul perception. I don't mean to equate solitariness with isolation. The wisdom of soul no longer belongs to anyone or any group, but is to be sought in the world itself — it must be sought consciously and thoughtfully and persistently in everyday life. There is indeed an intellectual dimension to this work; study is required, but the point is not study. At each step along the way, study must also be put aside in order to see and hear and feel how all of this soul work appears in the things of the world. Without study, the soul in the world remains closed; but without sacrificing what one has studied, that is, without releasing it, the soul in the world not only remains closed, the world disappears altogether.

This brings us to the point of having to say that the materialistic world, the world that presents itself as if soulless and that has come about as a result of the development of science and technology — that the materialistic world too can be seen as a movement of the soul. From the viewpoint of soul, the advance of materialism has the purpose not of removing soul but of giving soul solidity and substance. And here in America, where materialism has flowered and developed to the highest degree, the opportunity of facing the world with soul is greatest. It is quite amazing that all of the spiritual, magical, and soul traditions come from other places, not from America. The only tradition of soul work that is completely American is the American Indian shaman tradition, but it concentrates on nature. Because these traditions come from elsewhere, when one becomes involved in spiritual and psychological work, there always occurs an accompanying inner work, having to do with the fantasy that in order to experience soul one must go elsewhere — to the inner planes, to the higher levels, to the soul worlds, to the spirit worlds, always elsewhere. No one would suggest that the soul world is precisely this materialistic American world, that the work to be done is right here where soul is most readily available in the highly condensed form of what we like to call real things. Spiritually and psychologically we are still under invasion from the East, or from Europe. It may be that the tools for seeing through have been developed elsewhere, but the material to work on is right here — and not because it lacks soul and is in need of missionary work from afar, but because the material world may in fact be the culmination of the creating force of the soul of the world, its most highly developed form, the jewel of the world soul. This jewel is rough, uncut, unpolished, without radiance and glow, in need of work. But throwing it away would be to have no material. And without material — one makes up material to work on, makes an institution of the made-up material, and calls it inner work.

An example. These days there is a tremendous interest in abuse, and a procedure has now developed to seek out the early childhood abuse in the memories of those who find great difficulty in facing the world. Why can they not face the world? Well, the doctrine says, because of unresolved rage, of which they are not aware, but which is nonetheless held in unconscious memory. So one goes on an inner trip backward and revives the memory, locating the memory as if in the very tissues of the body. But the fact of the matter is that the body records, so to speak, any and all injuries. As far as the body is concerned a childhood fall from a swing, an accident, any trauma at all is retained and remembered

— as a hurt, but not with the consciousness of the specific event of hurt. Cellular memory or consciousness does not have the same form as wide awake consciousness. So when one begins to be told stories of early child abuse, the cellular consciousness finds one story as congenial as another; consequently, when collective stories begin to be told of how we were all abused children, every hurt in the body now has a fantasy. And then, further, when one hears that these early wounds result in co-dependency, alcoholism, drug abuse, sex addiction, or a thousand other forms of addiction — well, what is one to do? Enter into a twelve-step program, of course. Become an anonymous, collect in meetings and rooms and talk about oneself, turn away from the world and become a better person. Nowhere is it pointed out that the presenting difficulties may well be an indication that the world is becoming harder and harder to face without soul, that the abundance of soul in the world is a real killer when it is not faced with soul. Instead, the aim centers on becoming sweet and innocent, or letting the inner child now face the world in its naivete, without imaginal intelligence and image consciousness. Turn yourself over to another group, another seminar, another workshop, but do not turn yourself toward the world.

Does it not become apparent that the hermetic task of serving the soul of the world requires cunning, trickery, lightning swift intuition, constant mobility of imagination, in order to avoid on the one side the traps of the inner psychic journey and on the other the traps of unreflecting, unimaginative, stuck materialism, and to avoid the traps while remaining in their midst? The hermetic venture, because it involves theft and revolution, needs to be distinguished from the theft of Prometheus and the revolutionary tactics of Dionysus. Prometheus steals fire from the gods and gives it to man, and that theft brings about the establishment of human civilization. But it is a one-way theft, cutting mortals off from the gods and goddesses, setting the direction of making a world without the element of soul. The Hermetic theft, I suggest, is more fruitful because it provides a way of constant movement of imagination, the making of soul culture that renews rather than depletes the world. And while the Dionysian revolution brings change to world order through radical disruption that destroys, the action of hermetic world imagination brings about change in the order of things, constant change. For Dionysus, soul must be remembered at all costs, even if that entails the dismemberment of the old order. Hermetic disruption is a revolution from within, seeing that soul has not been exiled to some faraway place but that the place of exile is always right before us. Facing the world with soul means approaching the world with soul as well as finding it already there.

In Lieu of References

DEAR FRIEND,

Since the purpose of these letters has not been to exhibit a non-existent erudition but always to try and point to the world as teacher, I do not wish to send you off to read the invaluable books that have through the years stimulated and formed my imagination. I will, however, name some books you might also pass through as itinerant travelers seeking soul.

The writings of James Hillman
Stephan Hoeller, *Jung and the Lost Gospels*
Rudolf Steiner, *Isis and Sophia*
Anonymous, *Meditations on the Tarot*
R. J. Stewart, *Living Magical Arts*
Apuleius, *The Golden Ass*
Georg Kuhlewind, *From Normal to Healthy*
Gaston Bachelard, *The Poetics of Space*
Francis Ponge, *The Sun Placed in the Abyss and Other Texts*
Plato, *The Timaeus*
Vincent Scully, *The Earth, the Temple, and the Gods*
Donald Cowan, *Unbinding Prometheus: Education for the Coming Age*
Richard Palmer, *Hermeneutics*
Robert Sardello, *Educating with Soul*
Victor Bott, *Anthroposophical Medicine*
E. Douglas Hume, *Bechamp or Pasteur?*
Alan Cantwell, Jr., *AIDS: The Mystery and the Solution*
John Lash, *The Seeker's Handbook*

John Lash, *A Recreation of the Alchemical Mystery (unpublished)*
Franz Hartmann, *The Life and Doctrines of Paracelsus*
Walter Weisskopf, *Alienation and Economics*
Rudolf Steiner, *World Economy*
Robert Sardello and Randolph Severson, *Money and the Soul of the World*
Lewis Hyde, *The Gift: Imagination and the Erotic Life of Property*
Hazel Henderson, *Politics of the Solar Age*
Marshall McCluhan, *Understanding Media*
Ernst Lehrs, *Man or Matter*
Joseph Weizenbaum, *Computer Power and Human Reason*
Luke Howard, *On the Modification of Clouds*
The writings of Gertrude Stein
The writings of Ernest Fenollosa
Jorges Luis Borges, *Tlon*
Matisse, *Jazz*
Eric Gill, *Beauty Looks after Herself*
Robert Edmund Jones, *The Dramatic Imagination*
Rudolf Steiner, *Color*
Gerhardt Schmidt, *The Dynamics of Nutrition*
M. E. Jacobs, *Six Thousand Years of Bread*
Frank Norris, *The Octopus*
Pierre Janet, *Psychological Healing*
Euripides, *The Bacchae*
Empedocles, *Fragments*
Marcel Detienne, *Dionysos at Large*
Rudolf Steiner, *Wonders of the World*
The Homeric Hymn to Hermes
Karl Kerenyi, *Hermes - Guide of Souls*
Jenny Strauss Clay, *The Politics of Olympus*
Wolfram von Eschenbach, *Parzival*
Elmire Zolla, *Imagination*
Kathleen Raine, *Poetry and the Frontiers of Consciousness*

ARCHETYPAL IMAGINATION
Glimpses of the Gods in Life and Art

Noel Cobb

This unique book is about freeing psychology's poetic imagination
from the dead weight of unconscious assumptions about the soul.
Whether we think of the soul scientifically or medically, behaviorally or
in terms of inner development, all of us are used to thinking of it in an
individual context, as something personal. In this book, however, we are
asked to consider psychology from a truly transpersonal perspective as a
cultural, universal-human phenomenon.

Reading these essays we are taught to look at the world as the record of
the soul's struggles to awaken, as the soul's poetry. From this point of
view, the true basis of the mind is poetic. Beauty, love, and creativity are
as much instincts of the soul as sexuality or hunger. Thus these essays
praise the value and nobility of the imagination, and instead of the usual
masters of psychology the exemplars here are the artists and mystics of
the Western tradition: Dante, Rumi, Rilke, Munch, Lorca, Schumann,
Tarkovsky.

"I like Noel Cobb's outcries on behalf of ferocity, loneliness, anxiety, 'the hideous hag of life,'
beauty sitting in the lap of terror, Edvard Munch's paintings and Garcia Lorca's panther-
like poems — let's have more."   — **Robert Bly**, author of *Iron John*

"Noel Cobb's taking psychology deep into the world of art, with a strong distaste for psy-
chological reductionism, is a remarkable contribution. . . . To track the heart and mind of
the artist struggling with imagery and with the challenges of life is to watch the protype of
an engagement with imagery that any of us might experience . . . In this richly stuffed book
Cobb takes psychology to the threshold and invites it into the world, where the artist is bold
enough to live, where its language may have more life and its images more independence."
       — **Thomas Moore,** author of *The Care of the Soul*

256 pp   ISBN 0-940262-47-9

GAIA: A WAY OF KNOWING

Political Implications of the New Biology

Edited by William Irwin Thompson

Thompson brings together a collection of essays on the *Gaia* hypothesis by such authors as atmospheric scientist James Lovelock, biologist Lynn Margulis, cybernetic biologist Henry Atlan, and others. The suggestion is that for the first time since Newton, we have the chance to create a new ecology of consciousness, the basis for a new political and economic order.

224pp

ISBN 0-940262-23-1

GAIA 2: EMERGENCE

The New Science of Becoming

Edited by William Irwin Thompson

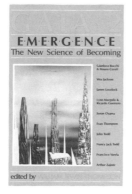

This exciting volume, bringing together an international gathering of scientists and philosophers concerned with the fate of our planet, hinges on the shift involved in considering *Gaia* no longer simply a *hypothesis* but a *theory* of evolution.

Based on a conference held in Perugia, Italy, this thought-provoking collection of papers and symposia confirms Heisenberg's saying that "real science" is made in the conversations of scientists. In it, we see what is perhaps the most important scientific idea of the twentieth century taking shape before our eyes.

Contributors include: James Lovelock & Lynn Margulis, Francisco Varela, Evan Thompson, Arthur Zajonc, Wes Jackson, John Todd and Nancy Jack Todd, Susan Oyama, Gianluca Bocchi and Mauro Ceruti.

WILLIAM IRWIN THOMPSON has edited the volume and contributed a substantial Introduction and Conclusion that point out the wider sociopolitical implications of this new way of thinking.

260pp

ISBN 0-940262-40-1

GAIASOPHY

*An Approach to Ecology based on Ancient Myth,
Spiritual Vision & Scientific Thinking*

Kees Zoeteman

Kees Zoeteman, a Dutch engineer and government environmentalist (Coordinator for National Environmental Planning), believes that ecology needs to be supplemented by *gaiasophy,* which he defines as "The knowledge and wisdom of the living Earth."

Zoeteman draws on practical experience married to a deep study of ancient myths and spiritual traditions regarding the earth's origins as well as on contemporary spiritual science. He argues that not until we fully understand the spiritual, as well as the physical anatomy of the earth *as a living being or organism*, shall we be able to address the vital environmental and social issues posed by the ecological crisis. On the basis of the most varied scientific and spiritual sources, Zoetemann then presents an evolutionary cosmology of the living being Earth. He proposes that we consider the earth truly "alive": the forests and grasslands as the respiratory system, the waters as the circulatory system, etc. Then he goes on to a consideration of the ways in which the digestion of nutrients, the excretion of wastes, and the free flow of information are all parts of Gaia's loving, organic process. Add to this two brilliant final chapters indicating ways of thinking *gaiasophically* about how to heal urban and rural "diseases," and one begins to see there are quite other ways of thinking about ecological issues than those we are used to.

376 pp   ISBN 0-940262-43-6

For a free catalog or ordering information write or call:

LINDISFARNE PRESS
RR 4 Box 94 A1
Hudson, NY 12534
(518) 851-9155

ALSO AVAILABLE IN THE SAME SERIES

THE PLANETS WITHIN

The Astrological Psychology of Marsilio Ficino

Thomas Moore

Introduction by Noel Cobb

The Planets Within asks us to return to antiquity with new eyes, to avoid superstition and literalism and yet recover what has been lost of antique sensibility. It centers on one of the most psychological movements of the pre-scientific age: Renaissance Italy, where a group of inner Columbuses charted territories which still give us today a much needed sense of who we are and where we have come from, and the right routes to take towards fertile and unexplored places. Chief among these masters of the interior life was Marsilio Ficino, presiding genius of the Florentine Academy, who taught that all things exist in soul and must be lived in its light. This study of Ficino broadens and deepens our understanding of psyche, for Ficino was a doctor of soul, and his insights teach us the care and nurture of soul.

The reader turning to this book for knowledge and self-knowledge will be delighted to find it so instructive, enjoyable, and "user-friendly." With Tom Moore as guide you will feel at home in the marvelous world of Renaissance Hermetism, its psychological and astrological insights, its music, its madness. How much Moore knows and how generous he is in giving it to the reader. **-James Hillman**

In my library this volume takes its rightful place beside those other classics of archetypal psychology after Jung: James Hillman's Revisioning Psychology, *Patricia Berry's* Echo's Subtle Body, *and Mary Watkins'* Waking Dreams. **-Noel Cobb**

In his presentation of psychological insight and understanding informed by Renaissance astrology and musicology, Dr. Moore's clarity with complex matters is only topped by his wisdom. **-David Miller**

ISBN 0-940262-28-2 / 228pp